Taste of Home's
Ground Beef
COOKBOOK

PICTURED ABOVE AND ON THE COVER: Tasty Meat Pie (p. 44).

Delicious Appetizers, Main Dishes and More!

With 205 recipes to choose from in *Taste of Home's Ground Beef Cookbook*, you'll never be at a loss when you need to put something on the table in a hurry.

Not only is ground beef practical and versatile, it's also oh-so-easy to prepare! You can create meaty snacks, soups, main dishes and so much more. For example, this cookbook gives you more than 20 appetizers to curb your hunger or delight your guests. Stacey Atkinson of Rugby, North Dakota shares her Ground Beef Snack Quiches on page 10, and she knows from experience what a great appetizer these little treats make.

Along with soups, salads, sandwiches, main dishes and sides, you'll find casseroles and more than 30 skillet meals that cook up on the stovetop. Whether you're looking to beef up a weekday meal or special-occasion spread, *Taste of Home's Ground Beef Cookbook* provides many recipes to help you cook something wonderful. Wanda Orton of Emporia, Kansas says her Meat Loaf Wellington is a great way to dress up meat loaf when company comes. You'll find her tasty recipe on page 66.

How can we be sure this cookbook has the recipes you're looking for? Fellow cooks from across the country shared their families' favorites, and each recipe was prepared and taste-tested in our Test Kitchens. The recipes appeared in past issues of *Taste of Home* magazine and its "sister" publications. And we compiled a variety of the best ones in *Taste of Home's Ground Beef Cookbook* to ensure that you have a great selection of recipes to make in your own kitchen today!

Editor: Jean Steiner
Art Directors: Kathy Crawford, Catherine Fletcher
Executive Editor/Books: Heidi Reuter Lloyd
Senior Editor: Julie Schnittka
Associate Editor: Beth Wittlinger
Proofreader: Julie Blume Benedict
Editorial Assistant: Barb Czysz
Food Editor: Janaan Cunningham
Associate Food Editors: Coleen Martin, Diane Werner
Senior Recipe Editor: Sue A. Jurack
Recipe Editors: Janet Briggs, Mary King
Food Photography: Rob Hagen, Dan Roberts, Jim Wieland
Set Stylists: Julie Ferron, Stephanie Marchese, Sue Myers, Jennifer Bradley Vent

Food Stylists: Kristin Arnett, Sarah Thompson, Joylyn Trickel
Associate Set Stylist: Melissa Haberman
Photographers' Assistant: Lori Foy
Creative Director: Ardyth Cope
Senior Vice President/Editor in Chief: Catherine Cassidy
President: Barbara Newton
Chairman and Founder: Roy Reiman

Taste of Home's Ground Beef Cookbook
©2005 Reiman Media Group, Inc.
5400 S. 60th St., Greendale WI 53129
International Standard Book Number: 0-89821-462-9
Library of Congress Control Number: 2005933665
All rights reserved.
Printed in U.S.A.

Contents

Appetizers
& Snacks

Chapter 1

Appetizer Meatballs

(Pictured below)

Nathalie Wiedmann-Guest, Caledon, Ontario

These are a favorite at parties and gatherings. The recipe is easy...and the meatballs can be made well ahead of time and frozen until needed. I think what makes them taste so good is the sauce.

    2 eggs, lightly beaten
    1 cup (4 ounces) shredded mozzarella
      cheese
  1/2 cup dry bread crumbs
  1/4 cup finely chopped onion
    2 tablespoons grated Parmesan cheese
    1 tablespoon ketchup
    2 teaspoons Worcestershire sauce
    1 teaspoon Italian seasoning
    1 teaspoon dried basil
    1 teaspoon salt
  1/4 teaspoon pepper
    2 pounds ground beef
SAUCE:
    1 bottle (14 ounces) hot and spicy *or*
      regular ketchup
    2 tablespoons cornstarch
    1 jar (12 ounces) apple jelly
    1 jar (12 ounces) currant jelly

In a bowl, combine the first 11 ingredients; add beef and mix well. Shape into 1-in. balls. Place on a rack in a shallow roasting pan. Bake at 350° for 10-15 minutes. Remove meatballs and rack; drain. Combine ketchup and cornstarch in roasting pan. Stir in jellies; add meatballs. Cover; bake 30 minutes or until beef is no longer pink. **Yield:** about 8 dozen.

Blue-Ribbon Beef Nachos

Diane Hixon, Niceville, Florida

Chili powder and salsa season a zesty mixture of ground beef and refried beans that's sprinkled with green onions, tomatoes and ripe olives. My family thinks these are the best nachos ever!

    1 pound ground beef
    1 small onion, chopped
    1 can (16 ounces) refried beans
    1 jar (16 ounces) salsa
    1 can (6 ounces) pitted ripe olives,
      chopped
  1/2 cup shredded cheddar cheese
    1 green onion, chopped
    2 tablespoons chili powder
    1 teaspoon salt
Tortilla chips
Sliced ripe olives, chopped green onions and
    tomatoes, optional

In a skillet, cook the beef and onion over medium heat until meat is no longer pink; drain. Stir in the next seven ingredients; heat through. Serve over tortilla chips. Top with olives, onions and tomatoes if desired. **Yield:** 6 servings.

Hot Beef Dip

Sonja Hanks, Snyder, Texas

This meaty appetizer really reflects the Lone Star State. As a busy science teacher, I find that cooking with ground beef fits nicely into my schedule.

    1 pound ground beef
  2/3 cup chopped onion
  1/2 cup chopped green pepper
    3 to 4 garlic cloves, minced
    1 can (8 ounces) tomato sauce
  1/4 cup ketchup
    1 teaspoon sugar
  3/4 teaspoon dried oregano
  1/4 teaspoon pepper

1 package (8 ounces) cream cheese,
  softened
1/4 cup grated Parmesan cheese
Tortilla chips

In a large skillet, cook beef, onion, green pepper and
garlic over medium heat until meat is no longer pink.
Add the tomato sauce, ketchup, sugar, oregano and
pepper; simmer for 10 minutes. Remove from the
heat and stir in cheeses until melted.

Transfer to a fondue pot or slow cooker; serve
warm with tortilla chips. **Yield:** 16-20 servings.

Mini Crescent Burgers

Pam Buhr, Mexico, Missouri

*A friend first brought these snacks to a Sunday school
party. The original recipe called for pork sausage, but I
substituted ground beef with taste-tempting results.*

1 **pound ground beef**
1 **cup (4 ounces) shredded cheddar
  cheese**
1 **envelope onion soup mix**
3 **tubes (8 ounces** *each***) refrigerated
  crescent rolls**

In a skillet, cook beef over medium heat until no
longer pink; drain. Stir in the cheese and soup mix;
set aside.

Separate crescent dough into triangles; cut each
triangle in half lengthwise, forming two triangles.
Place 1 tablespoon of the beef mixture along the
wide end of each triangle. Roll up; place pointed
side down 2 in. apart on ungreased baking sheets.
Bake at 375° for 15 minutes or until golden brown.
Yield: 4 dozen.

Corn Bread Pizza Wheels

(Pictured above right and on page 4)

Patrick Lucas, Cochran, Georgia

*This hearty, colorful snack looks like you fussed, but
it's simple to make. It's great for get-togethers.*

1 **pound ground beef**
1 **can (16 ounces) kidney beans, rinsed
  and drained**

1 **can (8 ounces) tomato sauce**
4 **teaspoons chili powder**
1 **jar (4 ounces) diced pimientos,
  drained**
1 **can (4 ounces) chopped green chilies,
  drained**
1 **cup (4 ounces) shredded cheddar
  cheese**
2 **tablespoons cornmeal**
2 **tubes (11-1/2 ounces** *each***) refrigerated
  corn bread twists**
Shredded lettuce, sliced tomatoes and sour
  cream

In a skillet, cook the beef over medium heat until no
longer pink; drain. Add the beans, tomato sauce
and chili powder. Simmer, uncovered, until the liquid has evaporated. Remove from the heat and
cool. Stir in the pimientos, chilies and cheese; set
aside.

Sprinkle two greased 14-in. pizza pans with cornmeal. Pat the corn bread dough into a 14-in. circle
on each pan. With a knife, cut a 7-in. X in the center of the dough. Cut another 7-in. X to form eight
pie-shaped wedges in the center. Spoon the filling
around the edge of dough. Fold points of dough
over filling; tuck under ring and pinch to seal (filling will be visible).

Bake at 400° for 15-20 minutes or until golden
brown. Fill center with lettuce, tomatoes and sour
cream. **Yield:** 2 pizzas (8 servings each).

ing powder and salt. Cut in shortening until the mixture resembles coarse crumbs. Gradually add water, tossing with a fork until a ball forms.

Divide dough in half. Roll out one portion into a 15-in. x 10-in. rectangle; transfer to an ungreased 15-in. x 10-in. x 1-in. baking pan. Spoon meat mixture over dough. Roll out the remaining dough into a 15-in. x 10-in. rectangle; place over filling. Bake at 425° for 25 minutes or until golden brown. Cut into small squares. **Yield:** about 10 dozen.

Poppy Seed Squares

(Pictured above)

Jo Baden, Independence, Kansas

When I came across this unusual appetizer, I just knew I had to try it. Although I make these squares every Christmas, no one tires of them.

1 pound ground beef
1-1/2 cups finely chopped fresh mushrooms
1 medium onion, finely chopped
1 can (10-3/4 ounces) condensed cream of celery *or* mushroom soup, undiluted
1 tablespoon prepared horseradish
1 teaspoon salt
1/2 teaspoon pepper
CRUST:
3 cups all-purpose flour
2 tablespoons poppy seeds
3/4 teaspoon baking powder
3/4 teaspoon salt
1 cup shortening
1/2 cup cold water

In a skillet, cook beef, mushrooms and onion over medium heat until meat is no longer pink; drain. Add the soup, horseradish, salt and pepper; mix well. Remove from the heat and set aside.

In a bowl, combine the flour, poppy seeds, bak-

Zucchini Pizza Bites

Cathy Dawe, Kent, Ohio

When we had a vegetable garden, I was constantly looking for ways to use my ample supply of zucchini. In this family-favorite recipe, zucchini is used to make a garden-fresh crust.

4 cups shredded unpeeled zucchini, drained and squeezed dry
1 cup (4 ounces) shredded cheddar cheese, *divided*
1 cup (4 ounces) shredded mozzarella cheese, *divided*
2 eggs, beaten
1 pound ground beef
1 medium onion, chopped
1/4 teaspoon salt
1/4 teaspoon garlic salt
1 can (8 ounces) tomato sauce
2 teaspoons dried oregano
1 medium green pepper, julienned
5 medium fresh mushrooms, sliced
1/3 cup grated Parmesan cheese

In a bowl, combine the zucchini, 1/2 cup cheddar cheese, 1/2 cup mozzarella cheese and eggs; mix well. Press onto the bottom and up the sides of a

About Ground Beef

Ground beef comes from a combination of beef cuts. But it may be used as a generic term to describe ground meat from a specific cut of beef, including chuck, round and sirloin. The label on the meat's package may specify the beef cut from which the product is ground.

greased 15-in. x 10-in. x 1-in. baking pan. Bake at 400° for 20-25 minutes or until crust is set and lightly browned.

Meanwhile, in a skillet, cook beef, onion, salt and garlic salt over medium heat until meat is no longer pink; drain. Stir in tomato sauce and oregano; mix well. Spoon over crust. Sprinkle with the green pepper, mushrooms, Parmesan cheese and remaining cheddar and mozzarella.

Bake at 400° for 15 minutes or until golden brown. Let stand 5 minutes before cutting. Cut into 2-in. squares. **Yield:** about 3 dozen.

Korean Wontons

Christy Lee, Horsham, Pennsylvania

These fried dumplings, filled with vegetables and beef, are very easy to prepare.

> 2 cups shredded cabbage
> 1 cup canned bean sprouts
> 1/2 cup shredded carrots
> 1-1/2 teaspoons plus 2 tablespoons vegetable oil, *divided*
> 1/3 pound ground beef
> 1/3 cup sliced green onions
> 1-1/2 teaspoons sesame seeds, toasted
> 1-1/2 teaspoons minced fresh gingerroot
> 3 garlic cloves, minced
> 1-1/2 teaspoons sesame oil
> 1/2 teaspoon salt
> 1/2 teaspoon pepper
> 1 package (12 ounces) wonton wrappers
> 1 egg, lightly beaten
> 3 tablespoons water

In a wok or large skillet, stir-fry cabbage, bean sprouts and carrots in 1-1/2 teaspoons oil until tender; set aside. In a small skillet, cook beef over medium heat until no longer pink; drain. Add to the vegetable mixture. Stir in the onions, sesame seeds, ginger, garlic, sesame oil, salt and pepper.

Place about 1 tablespoon of filling in the center of each wonton wrapper; keep other wonton wrappers covered until ready to use. Combine egg and water. Moisten wonton edges with egg mixture; fold opposite corners over filling and press to seal. Heat remaining vegetable oil in a large skillet. Cook wontons in batches for 1-2 minutes on each side or until golden brown, adding additional oil if needed. **Yield:** 5 dozen.

Taco Appetizer Platter

(Pictured below)

Iola Egle, McCook, Nebraska

A crowd usually gathers when I set out a platter full of my barbecue-flavored taco dip with corn chips. It's gone before I know it!

> 1-1/2 pounds ground beef
> 1/2 cup water
> 1 envelope taco seasoning
> 2 packages (8 ounces *each*) cream cheese, softened
> 1/4 cup milk
> 1 can (4 ounces) chopped green chilies, drained
> 2 medium tomatoes, seeded and chopped
> 1 cup chopped green onions
> 1-1/2 cups chopped lettuce
> 1/2 to 3/4 cup honey barbecue sauce
> 1 to 1-1/2 cups shredded cheddar cheese
> Large corn chips

In a skillet, cook beef over medium heat until no longer pink; drain. Add water and taco seasoning; simmer for 5 minutes.

In a bowl, combine the cream cheese and milk; spread on a 14-in. serving platter or pizza pan. Top with meat mixture. Sprinkle with chilies, tomatoes, onions and lettuce. Drizzle with barbecue sauce. Sprinkle with cheddar cheese. Serve with corn chips. **Yield:** 8-10 servings.

Ground Beef Snack Quiches

(Pictured below)

Stacey Atkinson, Rugby, North Dakota

A hearty appetizer like these meaty mini quiches is a perfect way to start a meal. They taste super made with ground beef, but I sometimes substitute bacon, ham, ground pork or sausage.

  1/4 **pound ground beef**
  1/8 **to 1/4 teaspoon garlic powder**
  1/8 **teaspoon pepper**
    1 **cup biscuit/baking mix**
  1/4 **cup cornmeal**
  1/4 **cup cold butter**
    2 **to 3 tablespoons boiling water**
    1 **egg**
  1/2 **cup half-and-half cream**
    1 **tablespoon chopped green onion**
    1 **tablespoon chopped sweet red pepper**
  1/8 **to 1/4 teaspoon salt**
  1/8 **to 1/4 teaspoon cayenne pepper**
  1/2 **cup finely shredded cheddar cheese**

In a saucepan, cook the beef, garlic powder and pepper over medium heat until meat is no longer pink; drain and set aside. In a bowl, combine the biscuit mix and cornmeal; cut in the butter. Add enough water to form a soft dough. Press onto the bottom and up the sides of greased miniature muffin cups.

Place teaspoonfuls of beef mixture into each shell. In a bowl, combine the egg, cream, onion, red pepper, salt and cayenne; pour over beef mixture. Sprinkle with cheese.

Bake at 375° for 20 minutes or until a knife inserted near the center comes out clean. **Yield:** 1-1/2 dozen.

Cranberry Meatballs

Joyce Bentley, Redlands, California

Cranberry sauce and brown sugar create a tangy glaze for moist meatballs that are good as an appetizer or as a main dish over rice. We love them so much, I prepare them year-round.

    2 **eggs**
    1 **envelope onion soup mix**
  1/2 **cup seasoned bread crumbs**
  1/4 **cup chopped dried cranberries**
    2 **tablespoons minced fresh parsley**
1-1/2 **pounds ground beef**
SAUCE:
    1 **can (16 ounces) whole-berry cranberry sauce**
  3/4 **cup ketchup**
  1/2 **cup beef broth**
    3 **tablespoons brown sugar**
    3 **tablespoons finely chopped onion**
    2 **teaspoons cider vinegar**

In a bowl, combine eggs, soup mix, bread crumbs, cranberries and parsley. Crumble beef over mixture and mix well. Shape into 1-in. balls; place 12 to 14 balls on a microwave-safe plate.

Cover with waxed paper; microwave on high for 3-4 minutes or until no longer pink. Remove to paper towels to drain. Repeat with remaining meatballs.

In a 2-qt. microwave-safe dish, combine all of the sauce ingredients. Cover and microwave on high for 3-4 minutes or until heated through, rotating once. Gently stir in the meatballs. Cover and cook on high for 1-2 minutes or until heated through. **Yield:** about 3 dozen.

Editor's Note: This recipe was tested in an 850-watt microwave.

Ranch Mushroom Dip

Barbara Harms, Valentine, Nebraska

Instead of the traditional sour cream base, this dip calls for French onion dip seasoned with ranch salad dressing mix.

- 2 packages (8 ounces *each*) cream cheese, softened
- 1 carton (8 ounces) French onion dip
- 1 envelope ranch salad dressing mix
- 1 pound ground beef
- 1/4 cup water
- 1 envelope taco seasoning
- 1 large tomato, chopped
- 2 cups (8 ounces) shredded cheddar cheese
- 1 medium onion, chopped
- 1 cup sliced fresh mushrooms
- 1 can (2-1/4 ounces) sliced ripe olives, drained

Tortilla chips

In a small mixing bowl, combine the first three ingredients; beat until smooth. Spread on a 12-in. or 14-in. serving plate. Refrigerate for 1 hour.

In a skillet, cook beef over medium heat until no longer pink; drain. Add water and taco seasoning; cook and stir for 5 minutes. Cool completely. Spread over the cream cheese layer. Refrigerate.

Just before serving, sprinkle with tomato, cheddar cheese, onion, mushrooms and olives. Serve with chips. **Yield:** about 8 cups.

Pronto Mini Pizzas

(Pictured above right)

Debbi Smith, Crossett, Arkansas

These quick savory pizzas on pita bread crusts are an excellent snack anytime.

- 1 pound ground beef
- 1 cup sliced fresh mushrooms
- 1/2 cup chopped green pepper
- 1/2 cup chopped onion
- 2 garlic cloves, minced
- 1 can (8 ounces) tomato sauce
- 1 teaspoon fennel seed
- 1/2 teaspoon salt
- 1/2 teaspoon dried oregano
- 4 pita breads
- 1 cup (4 ounces) shredded mozzarella cheese

In a skillet, cook the beef, mushrooms, green pepper, onion and garlic over medium heat until meat is no longer pink and the vegetables are tender; drain. Stir in the tomato sauce, fennel, salt and oregano. Simmer for 1-2 minutes.

Meanwhile, warm pitas in the microwave. Top each with meat mixture; sprinkle with cheese. Microwave or broil until cheese is melted. Cut into quarters. **Yield:** 4 servings.

Cold or Hot?

When attending potluck suppers, it's best to select a cold appetizer that can be prepared ahead and taken in a covered container. Hot appetizers requiring last-minute preparation are best served from your own kitchen.

Beef 'n' Egg Pockets

(Pictured below)

Kathy Vail, Canavoy, Prince Edward Island

My mother shared the recipe for these hand-held snacks that disappear whenever I make them. For added flavor, I sometimes toss in sliced fresh mushrooms or chopped green pepper.

2 cups all-purpose flour
2-1/2 teaspoons baking powder
1 teaspoon salt
2/3 cup shortening
2/3 cup milk
FILLING:
1/2 pound ground beef
1 medium onion, chopped
1 medium tomato, seeded and chopped
1 hard-cooked egg, finely chopped
Salt and pepper to taste

In a bowl, combine the flour, baking powder and salt; cut in shortening until the mixture resembles coarse crumbs. Gradually add milk, tossing with a fork until a ball forms. Cover and refrigerate.

Meanwhile, in a skillet, cook beef and onion over medium heat until meat is no longer pink; drain. Add the tomato, egg, salt and pepper; mix well.

Roll out pastry into an 18-in. x 9-in. rectangle; cut into 3-in. squares. Place a rounded tablespoonful of filling in center of each square. Fold in half, forming triangles; crimp edges to seal. Place on greased baking sheets. Bake at 400° for 15-20 minutes or until golden brown. **Yield:** 1-1/2 dozen.

Nacho Rice Dip

Audra Hungate, Holt, Missouri

Spanish rice mix adds an interesting twist to this effortless appetizer. Every time I serve this dip at get-togethers, my guests gobble it up.

1 package (6.8 ounces) Spanish rice and vermicelli mix
2 tablespoons butter
2 cups water
1 can (14-1/2 ounces) diced tomatoes, undrained
1 pound ground beef
1 pound (16 ounces) process cheese (Velveeta), cubed
1 can (14-1/2 ounces) stewed tomatoes
1 jar (8 ounces) process cheese sauce
Tortilla chips

In a large saucepan, cook rice mix in butter until golden. Stir in water and diced tomatoes; bring to a boil. Reduce heat; cover and simmer for 15-20 minutes or until rice is tender.

Meanwhile, in a skillet, cook beef over medium heat until no longer pink. Drain and add to the rice. Stir in cheese, stewed tomatoes and cheese sauce; cook and stir until cheese is melted.

Transfer to a slow cooker; cover and keep warm on low. Serve with tortilla chips. **Yield:** about 8 cups.

Hawaiian Roll-Ups

Ethel Lenters, Sioux Center, Iowa

These roll-ups were served at my baby shower luncheon many years ago. Pineapple, ham and bacon give them a tasty tropical twist.

1/2 cup milk
1 teaspoon prepared mustard

3 drops Worcestershire sauce
1 cup soft bread crumbs
2/3 cup packed brown sugar
1 teaspoon dried minced onion
1 teaspoon salt
1/4 teaspoon pepper
1-1/2 pounds ground beef
14 thin slices deli ham
14 bacon strips, halved widthwise
1 can (8 ounces) pineapple tidbits, undrained

In a bowl, combine the first eight ingredients. Crumble beef over the mixture and mix well. Spread beef mixture over ham slices. Roll up, starting with a short side. Cut in half widthwise; wrap a bacon slice around each. Secure with toothpicks.

Place in an ungreased 13-in. x 9-in. x 2-in. baking dish. Pour pineapple over roll-ups. Cover and bake at 375° for 30 minutes. Uncover; bake 30 minutes longer or until heated through and beef is no longer pink. **Yield:** 28 roll-ups.

Mushroom Burger Cups

Lucille Metcalfe, Barrie, Ontario

For many years on Christmas Eve, a dear friend would bring these hearty snacks to share with us and our six children. Now our grandchildren like to nibble on these treats as well.

18 slices bread, crusts removed
1/4 cup butter, softened
1 pound ground beef, cooked and drained
1 can (10-3/4 ounces) condensed cream of mushroom soup, undiluted
1 egg, beaten
1/2 cup shredded cheddar cheese
1/4 cup chopped onion
1 teaspoon Worcestershire sauce
Salt and pepper to taste

Using a biscuit cutter, cut 2-1/2-in. circles from bread slices. Spread butter over one side of each circle. Press circles, buttered side down, into ungreased miniature muffin cups.

In a bowl, combine all of the remaining ingredients and mix well. Spoon into the bread cups. Bake at 350° for 35 minutes or until golden brown. **Yield:** 1-1/2 dozen.

Beefy Biscuits

(Pictured above)

Kimberly Leddon, St. Marys, Georgia

On-the-go families will love these beefy treats. They're made in a wink with convenient refrigerated biscuits and a jar of prepared spaghetti sauce.

1 pound ground beef
1 jar (14 ounces) spaghetti sauce
2 tubes (8 ounces *each*) large refrigerated biscuits
1 cup (4 ounces) shredded cheddar cheese

In a skillet, cook beef over medium heat until no longer pink; drain. Stir in the spaghetti sauce; cook for 5-10 minutes or until heated through.

Press biscuits onto the bottom and up the sides of greased muffin cups. Spoon 2 tablespoonfuls meat mixture into the center of each cup. Bake at 375° for 15-17 minutes or until golden brown. Sprinkle with cheese; bake 3 minutes longer or until the cheese is melted. **Yield:** 8 servings.

Buying Beef

Look for ground beef that is bright red, avoiding any with brown or gray patches.

Cheesy Pizza Fondue

(Pictured below)

Julie Barwick, Mansfield, Ohio

While I was growing up, I would sit for hours reading cookbooks from cover to cover. I've carried that love of cooking with me through the years. I found this recipe when we lived in Wisconsin.

- 1/2 **pound ground beef**
- 1 **medium onion, chopped**
- 2 **cans (15 ounces *each*) pizza sauce**
- 1-1/2 **teaspoons dried basil *or* oregano**
- 1/4 **teaspoon garlic powder**
- 2-1/2 **cups (10 ounces) shredded sharp cheddar cheese**
- 1 **cup (4 ounces) shredded mozzarella cheese**

Breadsticks

In a heavy saucepan, cook beef and onion over medium heat until meat is no longer pink; drain. Stir in pizza sauce, basil and garlic powder; mix well. Reduce heat to low. Add cheeses; stir until melted.

Transfer to a slow cooker or fondue pot and keep warm over low heat. Serve with breadsticks. **Yield: about 5 cups.**

Hearty Cheese Dip

Jill Daly, Laramie, Wyoming

I've attended many cooking schools and written cookbooks. But I've found few appetizers that people enjoy as much as this recipe from my cousin.

- 1 **pound ground beef**
- 3/4 **cup chopped onion**
- 1/2 **cup chopped green pepper**
- 1 **garlic clove, minced**
- 1 **can (8 ounces) tomato sauce**
- 1/4 **cup ketchup**
- 1 **teaspoon sugar**
- 2-1/4 **teaspoons minced fresh oregano *or* 3/4 teaspoon dried oregano**
- 1/4 **teaspoon pepper**
- 1 **package (8 ounces) cream cheese, softened**
- 1/3 **cup grated Parmesan cheese**

Tortilla chips

In a skillet, cook the beef, onion, green pepper and garlic over medium heat until meat is no longer pink; drain. Stir in the tomato sauce, ketchup, sugar, oregano and pepper. Bring to a boil.

Reduce heat; cover and simmer for 10 minutes. Stir in cheeses. Cook and stir until cheese is melted. Serve hot with chips. **Yield: 4-1/2 cups.**

Easy Egg Rolls

Samantha Dunn, Leesville, Louisiana

I've always loved egg rolls, but every recipe I saw seemed too complicated. So I decided to start with a packaged coleslaw mix. Now I can make these yummy treats at a moment's notice.

- 1 **pound ground beef, cooked and drained**
- 1 **package (16 ounces) coleslaw mix**
- 2 **tablespoons soy sauce**
- 1/2 **teaspoon garlic powder**
- 1/4 **teaspoon ground ginger**

Onion powder to taste

- 2 **packages (16 ounces *each*) refrigerated egg roll wrappers**
- 1 **tablespoon all-purpose flour**

Vegetable oil for frying

In a bowl, combine the first six ingredients and mix well. Place a heaping tablespoonful of the beef

Step 1:
Place a rounded tablespoonful of filling in the center of each egg roll wrapper. Fold bottom corner of wrapper over filling.

Step 2:
Fold sides of wrapper over filling. Using a pastry brush, wet the top corner with a paste of flour and water.

Step 3:
Roll up tightly to seal, forming a tube.

---

mixture in the center of one egg roll wrapper. Fold the bottom corner over the filling. Fold the sides toward center over the filling.

In a small bowl, combine flour and enough water to make a paste. Moisten top corner with paste; roll up tightly to seal. Repeat.

In an electric skillet, heat 1 in. of oil to 375°. Fry egg rolls for 3-5 minutes or until golden brown. **Yield:** 40 egg rolls.

Editor's Note: Fill egg roll wrappers one at a time, keeping others covered until ready to use.

Veggie Nachos

Merry Holthus, Auburn, Nebraska

My family loves traditional nachos, but I was looking to offer something a little different. Now they gobble up this version with ground beef, vegetables and a creamy cheese sauce.

   1 **pound ground beef**
2-1/2 **quarts water,** *divided*

   1 **envelope taco seasoning**
   1 **medium bunch broccoli, broken into small florets**
   1 **medium head cauliflower, broken into small florets**
   1 **package (15-1/2 ounces) bite-size tortilla chips**
   1 **can (11 ounces) condensed nacho cheese soup, undiluted**
1/2 **cup milk**
1/4 **cup chopped sweet red pepper**
   1 **can (2-1/4 ounces) sliced ripe olives, drained**

In a skillet, cook beef over medium heat until no longer pink; drain. Add 3/4 cup water and taco seasoning. Simmer for 15 minutes.

Meanwhile, in a large saucepan, bring the remaining water to a boil. Add the broccoli and cauliflower. Cook for 2 minutes; drain. Place the chips on a large ovenproof serving platter. Top with the beef mixture, broccoli and cauliflower.

In a bowl, combine soup, milk and red pepper. Drizzle over vegetables. Sprinkle with olives. Bake at 350° for 10 minutes or until heated through. **Yield:** 12-16 servings.

Soups, Salads & Sandwiches

Chapter 2

are tender. Add the beans. Cover and simmer 15 minutes longer or until the beans are tender. **Yield:** 8 servings (2 quarts).

Beef Barley Soup

Lisa Otis, Drain, Oregon

This satisfying soup is wonderful for a busy day when you want something hot in a hurry. It makes a hearty meal with warm bread and a green salad.

- 2 **pounds ground beef**
- 2 **medium onions, chopped**
- 1/2 **cup chopped celery**
- 3 **cups water**
- 2 **cans (14-1/2 ounces *each*) beef broth**
- 1 **cup quick-cooking barley**
- 2 **cans (14-1/2 ounces *each*) diced tomatoes with garlic and onion, undrained**
- 2 **teaspoons Worcestershire sauce**
- 1 **teaspoon salt**
- 1 **teaspoon dried basil**

In a Dutch oven, cook beef, onions and celery over medium heat until meat is no longer pink and vegetables are tender; drain. Stir in the water and broth; bring to a boil.

Reduce heat. Add barley; cover and simmer for 10-20 minutes or until barley is tender. Stir in the remaining ingredients; heat through. Transfer to three 1-qt. freezer containers; cover and freeze for up to 3 months. **Yield:** 3 batches (3 quarts total).

To use frozen soup: Thaw in the refrigerator; place in a saucepan and heat through.

Hearty Hamburger Soup

(Pictured above)

Barbara Brown, Janesville, Wisconsin

At family get-togethers, our children always request this spirit-warming soup along with a fresh loaf of home-made bread. It has robust flavor, includes plenty of fresh-tasting vegetables and is easy to make.

- 1 **pound ground beef**
- 4 **cups water**
- 1 **can (14-1/2 ounces) diced tomatoes, undrained**
- 3 **medium carrots, sliced**
- 2 **medium potatoes, peeled and cubed**
- 1 **medium onion, chopped**
- 1/2 **cup chopped celery**
- 4 **beef bouillon cubes**
- 1-1/2 **teaspoons salt**
- 1/4 **teaspoon pepper**
- 1/4 **teaspoon dried oregano**
- 1 **cup cut fresh *or* frozen green beans**

In a large saucepan, cook beef over medium heat until no longer pink; drain. Add the next 10 ingredients; bring to a boil. Reduce heat; cover and simmer for 15 minutes or until potatoes and carrots

Pasta Pizza Soup

Linda Fox, Soldotna, Alaska

A steaming bowl of this soup hits the spot on a cold rainy or snowy day, which we have in abundance here. Oregano adds fast flavor to the pleasant combination of tender vegetables, pasta spirals and ground beef.

- 1 **pound ground beef**
- 4 **ounces fresh mushrooms, sliced**
- 1 **medium onion, chopped**

1 celery rib, thinly sliced
1 garlic clove, minced
4 cups water
1 can (14-1/2 ounces) Italian diced
  tomatoes, undrained
2 medium carrots, chopped
4 teaspoons beef bouillon granules
1 bay leaf
1-1/2 teaspoons dried oregano
1-1/2 cups cooked tricolor spiral pasta

In a large saucepan, cook beef, mushrooms, onion, celery and garlic over medium heat until meat is no longer pink and vegetables are tender; drain. Stir in water, tomatoes, carrots, bouillon, bay leaf and oregano. Bring to a boil.

Reduce heat; cover and simmer for 20-25 minutes or until carrots are tender. Stir in pasta; heat through. Discard bay leaf. **Yield:** 8 servings (about 2 quarts).

Meaty Garden Salad

Jo Jaquith, Marietta, Georgia

My sister-in-law originally made this filling salad. Over the years, I've modified it slightly, but it's still a favorite of the men in the family.

1 pound ground beef
1 garlic clove, minced
1 cup water
1 beef bouillon cube
1 cup instant rice
3 medium unpeeled cucumbers, cubed
4 plum tomatoes, cubed
2 celery ribs, sliced
1/2 cup sliced green onions
1/2 cup diced green pepper
Salt and pepper to taste
Salad dressing of your choice

In a skillet, cook beef and garlic over medium heat until meat is no longer pink; drain and set aside. In a saucepan, bring water and bouillon to a boil. Stir in rice; remove from the heat. Cover and let stand for 5 minutes or until tender.

Combine the rice and beef in a large bowl. Cover and refrigerate for 2 hours or until chilled. Add cucumbers, tomatoes, celery, onions, green pepper, salt and pepper; mix well. Serve with salad dressing. **Yield:** 12 servings.

Tex-Mex Pitas

(Pictured below)

Helen Overman, Pottsboro, Texas

I sometimes treat my friends at work to these peppy pitas at lunchtime. I prepare everything in advance, so the spicy sandwiches can just be zapped in the microwave to warm them up.

2 pounds ground beef
1 envelope taco seasoning
1/3 cup water
1 can (16 ounces) refried beans
1 can (10 ounces) diced tomatoes and
  green chilies, undrained
Pinch ground cumin
7 pita breads (6 inches), halved
3 cups (12 ounces) shredded cheddar
  cheese
Sliced jalapenos

In a skillet, cook beef over medium heat until no longer pink; drain. Stir in taco seasoning, water, beans, tomatoes and cumin. Simmer, uncovered, for 20 minutes, stirring occasionally.

Spoon about 1/3 cup into each pita half; top with about 2 tablespoons cheese and a few jalapeno slices. Place in an ungreased 13-in. x 9-in. x 2-in. baking pan. Bake at 350° for 10 minutes or until cheese is melted. **Yield:** 7 servings.

Corny Tomato Dumpling Soup

(Pictured below)

Jackie Ferris, Tiverton, Ontario

I have a big garden on our farm and enjoy cooking with my harvest. In this savory tomato soup, corn stars in both the broth and dumplings. It has a fresh-picked flavor. Ground beef makes it a hearty first course or satisfying light main dish.

- 1 pound ground beef
- 3 cups fresh *or* frozen corn
- 1 can (28 ounces) diced tomatoes, undrained
- 2 cans (14-1/2 ounces *each*) beef broth
- 1 cup chopped onion
- 1 garlic clove, minced
- 1-1/2 teaspoons dried basil
- 1-1/2 teaspoons dried thyme
- 1/2 teaspoon dried rosemary, crushed
- Salt and pepper to taste
- CORN DUMPLINGS:
- 1 cup all-purpose flour
- 1/2 cup cornmeal
- 2-1/2 teaspoons baking powder
- 1/2 teaspoon salt
- 1 egg
- 2/3 cup milk
- 1 cup fresh *or* frozen corn

- 1/2 cup shredded cheddar cheese
- 1 tablespoon minced fresh parsley

In a large saucepan or Dutch oven, cook beef over medium heat until no longer pink; drain. Stir in corn, tomatoes, broth, onion, garlic and seasonings. Bring to a boil. Reduce heat; cover and simmer for 30-45 minutes.

For dumplings, combine flour, cornmeal, baking powder and salt in a bowl. In another bowl, beat egg; stir in milk, corn, cheese and parsley. Stir into dry ingredients just until moistened.

Drop by tablespoonfuls onto simmering soup. Cover and simmer for 15 minutes or until a toothpick inserted in a dumpling comes out clean (do not lift cover while simmering). **Yield:** 8 servings (about 2 quarts).

Tortellini Soup

Marsha Farley, Bangor, Maine

This soup is delicious, pretty and unbelievably fast to make. For a creamy variation, I sometimes substitute cream of mushroom soup for the French onion soup.

- 1 pound ground beef
- 3-1/2 cups water
- 1 can (28 ounces) diced tomatoes, undrained
- 1 can (10-1/2 ounces) condensed French onion soup, undiluted
- 1 package (9 ounces) frozen cut green beans
- 1 package (9 ounces) refrigerated cheese tortellini
- 1 medium zucchini, chopped
- 1 teaspoon dried basil

In a large saucepan, cook beef over medium heat until no longer pink; drain. Add remaining ingredients and bring to a boil. Cook, uncovered, for 5 minutes or until heated through. **Yield:** 6-8 servings.

Tater Tot Taco Salad

Eleanor Mielke, Mitchell, South Dakota

Since I love potatoes and my husband and I both enjoy the flavor of tacos, this fun dish is a tasty meal-in-one for the two of us. It's not as messy as eating tacos...and the recipe can easily be doubled.

- 2 cups frozen miniature Tater Tots
- 1/2 pound ground beef
- 2 tablespoons taco seasoning
- 1/2 cup shredded cheddar cheese
- 1/4 cup sliced ripe *or* stuffed olives
- 1 cup shredded lettuce
- 2 tablespoons taco sauce
- 1/4 cup sour cream

Bake Tater Tots according to package directions. Meanwhile, in a large skillet, cook beef over medium heat until no longer pink; drain. Stir in taco seasoning.

Divide Tater Tots between two serving plates or bowls. Top with taco mixture, cheese, olives, lettuce, taco sauce and sour cream. **Yield:** 2 servings.

Cola Burgers

(Pictured at right)

Melva Baumer, Millmont, Pennsylvania

A friend who's an excellent cook shared this hamburger recipe with me, and it has since become a family favorite. The unusual combination of cola and French salad dressing added to the ground beef gives it fabulous flavor. The mixture is also used as a basting sauce on the moist burgers.

- 1 egg
- 1/2 cup cola, *divided*
- 1/2 cup crushed saltines (about 15)
- 6 tablespoons French salad dressing, *divided*
- 2 tablespoons grated Parmesan cheese
- 1/4 teaspoon salt
- 1-1/2 pounds ground beef
- 6 hamburger buns, split

Lettuce leaves
Tomato slices

In a bowl, combine the egg, 1/4 cup cola, cracker crumbs, 2 tablespoons salad dressing, Parmesan cheese and salt. Add beef and mix well. Shape into six 3/4-in.-thick patties (the mixture will be moist). In a bowl, combine the remaining cola and salad dressing; set aside.

Grill the patties, uncovered, over medium-hot heat for 3 minutes on each side. Brush with the

cola mixture and grill 8-10 minutes longer or until the meat juices run clear, basting and turning occasionally. Serve on buns with lettuce and tomato. **Yield:** 6 servings.

Editor's Note: Diet cola is not recommended for this recipe.

Meat Storage

Store ground beef in the coldest part of your refrigerator, which is likely your meat compartment. Use it within 1 to 2 days of purchase.

Uncooked ground beef can be frozen for 2 weeks in its original packaging. For highest quality, don't refreeze beef that has been frozen and defrosted.

Shape uncooked hamburger patties into uniform sizes, separate each with double layers of waxed paper, wrap and freeze. That way, you can easily remove as many patties as needed at a time.

for 8 hours or until heated through. **Yield:** 14 servings (3-1/2 quarts).

Savory Winter Soup

(Pictured above)

Dana Simmons, Lancaster, Ohio

Even my father, who doesn't particularly like soup, enjoys my full-flavored vegetable soup featuring ground beef.

> 2 pounds ground beef
> 3 medium onions, chopped
> 1 garlic clove, minced
> 3 cans (10-1/2 ounces *each*) condensed beef broth, undiluted
> 1 can (28 ounces) diced tomatoes, undrained
> 3 cups water
> 1 cup *each* diced carrots and celery
> 1 cup fresh *or* frozen cut green beans
> 1 cup cubed peeled potatoes
> 2 tablespoons minced fresh parsley *or* 2 teaspoons dried parsley flakes
> 1 teaspoon dried basil
> 1/2 teaspoon dried thyme
> Salt and pepper to taste

In a skillet, cook beef, onions and garlic over medium heat until the meat is no longer pink; drain. Transfer to a 5-qt. slow cooker. Add the remaining ingredients and mix well. Cover and cook on high

Meat Loaf Hamburgers

Sandi Pichon, Slidell, Louisiana

Everyone will rave about these tender, mellow-tasting hamburgers. They're a nice alternative to plain ground beef patties.

> 1 cup (8 ounces) sour cream
> 1-1/4 cups crushed cornflakes
> 1 tablespoon diced onion
> 1/2 to 1 teaspoon salt
> 1/8 teaspoon pepper
> 1-1/2 pounds ground beef
> 8 kaiser *or* hamburger buns, split
> **Lettuce leaves**
> **Tomato slices**

In a large bowl, combine the first five ingredients; add beef and mix well. Shape into eight patties. Grill, broil or pan-fry until the meat is no longer pink. Serve on buns with lettuce and tomato. **Yield:** 8 servings.

Corn Bread Salad

Sherry Edwards, Camden, Arkansas

This recipe appeared in our local newspaper years ago. I adapted the recipe to suit our tastes.

> 3/4 pound ground beef
> 1-1/2 cups crumbled corn bread
> 1 can (15 ounces) pinto beans, rinsed and drained
> 2 celery ribs, chopped
> 1 large onion, chopped
> 4 medium tomatoes, chopped
> **TOPPING:**
> 1-1/3 cups mayonnaise
> 2 teaspoons sugar
> 2 teaspoons vinegar

In a skillet, cook beef over medium heat until no longer pink; drain and cool slightly. In a large bowl, layer corn bread, beans, celery, onion and tomatoes. In a small bowl, combine the mayonnaise, sugar and vinegar; mix well. Spoon beef over tomato layer. Spread topping over salad (do not toss). **Yield:** 8 servings.

Spicy Cheeseburger Soup

Lisa Mast, White Cloud, Michigan

This creamy soup brings my family to the table in a hurry. I love the warming zip of cayenne.

- 1-1/2 cups water
- 2 cups cubed peeled potatoes
- 2 small carrots, grated
- 1 small onion, chopped
- 1/4 cup chopped green pepper
- 1 jalapeno pepper, seeded and chopped
- 1 garlic clove, minced
- 1 tablespoon beef bouillon granules
- 1/2 teaspoon salt
- 1 pound ground beef, cooked and drained
- 2-1/2 cups milk, *divided*
- 3 tablespoons all-purpose flour
- 8 ounces process cheese (Velveeta), cubed
- 1/4 to 1 teaspoon cayenne pepper, optional
- 1/2 pound sliced bacon, cooked and crumbled

In a large saucepan, combine the first nine ingredients; bring to a boil. Reduce heat; cover and simmer for 15-20 minutes or until potatoes are tender. Stir in beef and 2 cups milk; heat through.

Combine flour and remaining milk until smooth; gradually stir into soup. Bring to a boil; cook and stir for 2 minutes or until thickened and bubbly. Reduce heat; stir in cheese until melted. Add cayenne if desired. Top with bacon just before serving. **Yield:** 6-8 servings (about 2 quarts).

Editor's Note: When cutting or seeding hot peppers, use rubber or plastic gloves to protect your hands. Avoid touching your face.

Sombrero Pasta Salad

(Pictured at right)

Patty Ehlen, Burlington, Wisconsin

I take this slightly spicy salad to almost every party or picnic I attend. Every time, I come home with lots of compliments, but never any leftovers! Folks always go back for seconds, sometimes thirds.

- 1 package (16 ounces) spiral pasta
- 1 pound ground beef
- 3/4 cup water
- 1 envelope taco seasoning
- 2 cups (8 ounces) shredded cheddar cheese
- 1 large green pepper, chopped
- 1 medium onion, chopped
- 1 medium tomato, chopped
- 2 cans (2-1/4 ounces *each*) sliced ripe olives, drained
- 1 bottle (16 ounces) Catalina *or* Western salad dressing

Cook pasta according to package directions. Meanwhile, in a skillet, cook beef over medium heat until no longer pink; drain. Add water and taco seasoning; simmer, uncovered, for 15 minutes.

Rinse pasta in cold water and drain; place in a large bowl. Add beef mixture, cheese, green pepper, onion, tomato and olives; mix well. Add the dressing and toss to coat. Cover and refrigerate for at least 1 hour. **Yield:** 10 servings.

Lasagna Soup

(Pictured below)

Gladys Shaffer, Elma, Washington

This recipe is excellent for working mothers because it's fast and very flavorful. Fresh zucchini and corn add color and crunch to a boxed lasagna dinner mix.

    1   pound ground beef
  1/2   cup chopped onion
    1   package (7-3/4 ounces) lasagna dinner
        mix
    5   cups water
    1   can (14-1/2 ounces) diced tomatoes,
        undrained
    1   can (7 ounces) whole kernel corn,
        undrained
    2   tablespoons grated Parmesan cheese
    1   small zucchini, chopped

In a Dutch oven or soup kettle, cook beef and onion over medium heat until meat is no longer pink; drain. Add contents of lasagna dinner sauce mix, water, tomatoes, corn and Parmesan cheese; bring to a boil. Reduce heat; cover and simmer for 10 minutes, stirring occasionally.

Add the lasagna noodles and zucchini. Cover and simmer for 10 minutes or until the noodles are tender. Serve immediately. **Yield:** 10 servings (2-1/2 quarts).

Italian Tortellini Salad

Kelly Schmitz Mapes, Fort Collins, Colorado

This original recipe includes flavors that family and friends savor. Serve it warm for dinner and chilled for potlucks.

    1   pound ground beef
    1   envelope Italian salad dressing mix
  1/4   cup water
    1   package (19 ounces) frozen cheese
        tortellini, cooked and drained
    3   to 4 plum tomatoes, chopped
    1   medium zucchini, chopped
    1   cup (4 ounces) shredded mozzarella
        cheese
    2   tablespoons olive oil
    2   tablespoons red wine vinegar

In a skillet, cook beef over medium heat until no longer pink; drain. Add salad dressing mix and water. Bring to a boil. Reduce heat; simmer, uncovered, for 3 minutes.

In a large bowl, combine the tortellini, tomatoes, zucchini, cheese and beef mixture. Combine oil and vinegar; pour over salad and toss to coat. Serve immediately or refrigerate for at least 1 hour. **Yield:** 10 servings.

Simple Summer Salad

Carol Stone, Rankin, Illinois

Although my family is not big on salads, they love this version resembling seven-layer salad. We enjoy it on summer days when it's too hot to eat a big meal.

    1   pound ground beef
    3   cups torn lettuce
    2   cups (8 ounces) shredded cheddar
        cheese
    1   medium tomato, chopped
    1   small onion, chopped
    4   hard-cooked eggs, chopped
  1/2   to 3/4 cup mayonnaise
Salt and pepper to taste

In a skillet, cook beef over medium heat until no longer pink; drain. Cool for 5 minutes. In a large bowl, toss the lettuce, cheese, tomato, onion, eggs and beef. Add mayonnaise, salt and pepper; toss to coat. Serve immediately. **Yield:** 12 servings.

Hot Beef Cheddar Subs

Marann Reilly, Lithia Springs, Georgia

Hot Beef Cheddar Subs are like cheesy sloppy joes tucked into hollowed-out crusty rolls. My family devours these hearty and yummy sandwiches.

    4   submarine sandwich buns
    1   pound ground beef
    1   medium green pepper, diced
    1   small onion, diced
    1   can (10-3/4 ounces) condensed cheddar
        cheese soup, undiluted
    1/4 teaspoon Worcestershire sauce
    4   slices American cheese

Cut a thin slice off the top of each bun; set tops aside. Carefully hollow out bottoms, leaving a 1/2-in. shell. Set aside 1/2 cup bread. In a skillet, cook beef, green pepper and onion over medium heat until meat is no longer pink; drain. Stir in the soup, Worcestershire sauce and reserved bread; mix well.

Spoon into buns; top each with a cheese slice. Replace tops. Place on an ungreased baking sheet. Bake, uncovered, at 350° for 5-7 minutes or until cheese is melted. **Yield:** 4 servings.

Ground Beef Chili

(Pictured above right)

Shannon Wright, Erie, Pennsylvania

Everyone who tastes my chili comments that it is restaurant-quality. It's especially good with homemade corn bread. I have always enjoyed cooking and developing original recipes like this one.

    3   pounds ground beef
    1   large onion, chopped
    1   medium green pepper, chopped
    2   celery ribs, chopped
    2   cans (16 ounces *each*) kidney beans,
        rinsed and drained

    1   can (29 ounces) tomato puree
    1   jar (16 ounces) salsa
    1   can (14-1/2 ounces) diced tomatoes,
        undrained
    1   can (10-1/2 ounces) condensed beef
        broth, undiluted
    1   to 2 cups water
    1/4 cup chili powder
    2   tablespoons Worcestershire sauce
    1   tablespoon dried basil
    2   teaspoons ground cumin
    2   teaspoons steak sauce
    1   teaspoon garlic powder
    1   teaspoon salt
    1   teaspoon coarsely ground pepper
  1-1/2 teaspoons browning sauce, optional
Additional chopped onion, optional

In a Dutch oven, cook beef, onion, green pepper and celery over medium heat until meat is no longer pink and vegetables are tender; drain.

Stir in the beans, tomato puree, salsa, tomatoes, broth, water, seasonings and browning sauce if desired. Bring to a boil. Reduce heat; simmer, uncovered, for 30 minutes or until chili reaches desired thickness. Garnish with chopped onion if desired. **Yield:** 16 servings.

is tender. Garnish with cheese and tortilla chips. **Yield:** 8 servings (2 quarts).

Pronto Taco Soup

(Pictured above and on page 16)

Priscilla Gilbert, Indian Harbour Beach, Florida

When out-of-state friends dropped by, I invited them to stay for dinner, knowing that I could put together this mild, chili-flavored soup in a jiffy. I served it with corn-meal muffins and a crisp salad for a filling meal everyone loved. My guests even asked for the recipe!

       1 **pound ground beef**
       1 **medium onion, chopped**
       2 **garlic cloves, minced**
       2 **cans (14-1/2 ounces *each*) beef broth**
       1 **can (14-1/2 ounces) diced tomatoes, undrained**
 1-1/2 **cups picante sauce**
       1 **cup uncooked spiral *or* small shell pasta**
       1 **medium green pepper, chopped**
       2 **teaspoons chili powder**
       1 **teaspoon dried parsley flakes**
Shredded cheddar cheese and tortilla chips

In a large saucepan, cook beef, onion and garlic over medium heat until meat is no longer pink; drain. Add the broth, tomatoes, picante sauce, pasta, green pepper, chili powder and parsley.

Bring to a boil, stirring occasionally. Reduce heat; cover and simmer for 10-15 minutes or until pasta

Stroganoff in a Bun

Corrine Lingberg, Beresford, South Dakota

After just one taste, people love these sandwiches. They are great with deviled eggs and baked beans.

      2 **pounds ground beef**
      1 **large onion, chopped**
      1 **can (10-3/4 ounces) condensed cream of mushroom soup, undiluted**
      1 **cup mayonnaise**
    3/4 **cup finely chopped celery**
    2/3 **cup condensed cheddar cheese soup, undiluted**
     18 **hamburger buns, split**

In a large skillet, cook beef and onion over medium heat until meat is no longer pink; drain. Stir in the mushroom soup, mayonnaise, celery and cheese soup. Bring to a boil. Reduce heat; simmer, uncovered, for 10 minutes or until heated through. Serve on buns. **Yield:** 18 servings.

   Editor's Note: Reduced-fat or fat-free mayonnaise may not be substituted for regular mayonnaise in this recipe.

Make-Ahead Meatball Salad

Rexann LaFleur, Twin Falls, Idaho

I must admit when my husband's grandma served this, we were all a little leery. But the first bite was very convincing…and then we couldn't get enough of this tasty salad.

      1 **pound ground beef**
    1/2 **cup seasoned bread crumbs**
    1/2 **cup Italian salad dressing**
      6 **cups torn salad greens**
      1 **medium red onion, thinly sliced**
      1 **cup (4 ounces) shredded mozzarella cheese**
      1 **can (2-1/4 ounces) sliced ripe olives, drained**
Caesar Italian salad dressing *or* salad dressing of your choice

In a bowl, combine beef and bread crumbs. Shape into 3/4-in. balls. Place in a greased 8-in. square baking pan. Bake at 350° for 15-20 minutes or until meat is no longer pink; drain. Cool for 15-30 minutes. Place Italian salad dressing in a resealable plastic bag; add meatballs. Seal and refrigerate overnight.

Drain and discard marinade. On a serving platter or individual plates, arrange salad greens, onion, cheese and olives. Top with meatballs. Drizzle with dressing. **Yield:** 4 servings.

Super Sloppy Joes

(Pictured below right)

Ellen Stringer, Fairmont, West Virginia

Mother made these fresh-tasting sloppy joes many times when I was growing up. She passed the recipe on to me.

  2 pounds ground beef
1/2 cup chopped onion
  2 celery ribs with leaves, chopped
1/4 cup chopped green pepper
1-2/3 cups canned crushed tomatoes
1/4 cup ketchup
  2 tablespoons brown sugar
  1 tablespoon vinegar
  1 tablespoon Worcestershire sauce
  1 tablespoon steak sauce
1/2 teaspoon garlic salt
1/4 teaspoon ground mustard
1/4 teaspoon paprika
  8 to 10 hamburger buns, split

In a Dutch oven, cook beef, onion, celery and green pepper over medium heat until the meat is no longer pink and the vegetables are tender; drain. Add the next nine ingredients; mix well.

Simmer, uncovered, for 35-40 minutes, stirring occasionally. Spoon 1/2 cup meat mixture onto each bun. **Yield:** 8-10 servings.

Layered Chalupa Salad

Virginia Zeckser, Mode, Illinois

This favorite is always requested for various family occasions. Although it serves a lot of people, this zippy salad doesn't last long on our dinner table. The bowl is usually empty after one pass around.

  3 pounds ground beef
  1 can (16 ounces) refried beans
  1 can (16 ounces) kidney beans, rinsed
    and drained
1/2 cup water
1/4 cup cider vinegar
  2 tablespoons garlic salt
  1 teaspoon pepper
  1 can (8 ounces) tomato sauce
  1 teaspoon hot pepper sauce
Corn chips
Optional toppings: shredded cheddar cheese,
  shredded lettuce, chopped tomatoes,
  finely chopped radishes and sweet onion

In a Dutch oven, cook beef over medium heat until no longer pink; drain. Add beans, water, vinegar, garlic salt and pepper. Bring to a boil. Reduce heat; simmer, uncovered, for 30 minutes, stirring occasionally.

Meanwhile, in a saucepan, combine the tomato sauce and hot sauce; heat through. Place corn chips on a large serving platter; top with beef mixture and toppings of your choice. Drizzle with tomato sauce mixture. **Yield:** 14 servings.

Spicy Beef Salad

(Pictured below)

Natercia Yailaian, Somerville, Massachusetts

This delicious salad doesn't skimp on ingredients or flavor. I often make it on days when I'm especially pressed for time. My husband, my mother and I all rate it as a favorite.

- 1 pound ground beef
- 1/3 cup vegetable oil
- 3 tablespoons lime juice
- 2 tablespoons soy sauce
- 2 tablespoons molasses
- 1 small jalapeno pepper, seeded and minced
- 1 garlic clove, minced
- 3/4 teaspoon ground ginger
- 6 cups torn salad greens
- 1 large tomato, cut into wedges
- 2 green onions, sliced

Jalapeno pepper and lime slices, optional

In a skillet, cook beef over medium heat until no longer pink. Meanwhile, in a small bowl, combine oil, lime juice, soy sauce, molasses, jalapeno, garlic and ginger; mix well.

Drain the beef and add the oil mixture. Cook, uncovered, over medium heat for 5 minutes or until heated through. On a large platter, layer the salad greens, tomato, beef mixture and onions. Garnish with jalapeno and lime slices if desired. **Yield:** 8 servings.

Editor's Note: When cutting or seeding hot peppers, use rubber or plastic gloves to protect your hands. Avoid touching your face.

Beef and Bacon Chowder

Nancy Schmidt, Center, Colorado

Rave reviews are sure to follow when this creamy chowder appears on the table. Bacon makes it rich and hearty. It's popular with my whole family.

- 1 pound ground beef
- 2 cups chopped celery
- 1/2 cup chopped onion
- 4 cups milk
- 3 cups cubed peeled potatoes, cooked
- 2 cans (10-3/4 ounces *each*) condensed cream of mushroom soup, undiluted
- 2 cups chopped carrots, cooked

Salt and pepper to taste

- 12 bacon strips, cooked and crumbled

In a soup kettle or Dutch oven, cook the beef, celery and onion over medium heat until the meat is no longer pink and the celery and onion are tender; drain.

Add the milk, potatoes, soup, carrots, salt and pepper; heat through. Stir in the bacon just before serving. **Yield:** 12 servings (3 quarts).

Beef-Stuffed French Bread

Julie Scott, Pratt, Kansas

My husband, David, loves these tasty, satisfying sandwiches. The cheesy filling goes together in a jiffy.

- 1 unsliced loaf French bread (1 pound)
- 1 pound ground beef
- 1 can (10-3/4 ounces) condensed cheddar cheese soup, undiluted
- 1 medium green pepper, chopped
- 1 celery rib, chopped
- 1 tablespoon Worcestershire sauce
- 1 teaspoon salt
- 1/2 teaspoon pepper
- 4 slices process American cheese, halved

Cut off top of bread. Carefully hollow out bottom of loaf, leaving a 1/2-in. shell. Cut removed bread into small cubes; set aside.

In a skillet, cook beef over medium heat until no longer pink; drain. Add soup, green pepper, celery, Worcestershire sauce, salt and pepper. Cook and stir for 3-4 minutes. Stir in the reserved bread cubes.

Spread into bread shell. Top with cheese. Replace bread top. Place on an ungreased baking sheet. Bake at 350° for 6-8 minutes or until cheese is melted. **Yield:** 4 servings.

Hearty Spinach Salad

Rita Goshaw, South Milwaukee, Wisconsin

Ground beef turns an ordinary spinach salad into a main dish. Minced garlic adds just the right amount of zip. You can easily substitute any type of lettuce for the spinach.

  1 package (10 ounces) fresh spinach, torn
  1 pound ground beef, cooked and drained
  2 large tomatoes, cut into wedges
  2 cups (8 ounces) shredded sharp
     cheddar cheese
1/2 cup sliced fresh mushrooms
  6 garlic cloves, minced
Salt and pepper to taste
Salad dressing of your choice

In a large salad bowl, toss the spinach, beef, tomatoes, cheese, mushrooms, garlic, salt and pepper. Serve with salad dressing. **Yield:** 14 servings.

Pizza Hoagies

(Pictured above right)

Barbara Mery, Bothell, Washington

My husband and three sons love these crispy sandwiches filled with a moist pizza-flavored mixture. They're so popular, I frequently prepare them on weekends and double the recipe.

  1 pound ground beef
1/2 cup chopped onion
  1 can (15 ounces) pizza sauce
1/4 cup chopped ripe olives

  2 teaspoons dried basil
  1 teaspoon dried oregano
  8 hoagie *or* submarine sandwich buns *or*
     French rolls
  2 cups (8 ounces) shredded mozzarella
     cheese

In a skillet, cook beef and onion over medium heat until meat is no longer pink; drain. Stir in pizza sauce, olives, basil and oregano. Cook for 10 minutes or until heated through.

Cut 1/4 in. off the top of each roll; set aside. Carefully hollow out bottom of roll, leaving a 1/4-in. shell (discard removed bread or save for another use). Sprinkle 2 tablespoons cheese inside each shell. Fill each with about 1/2 cup meat mixture. Sprinkle with remaining cheese, gently pressing down to flatten. Replace bread tops.

Individually wrap four sandwiches tightly in foil; freeze for up to 3 months. Place remaining sandwiches on a baking sheet. Bake at 375° for 15 minutes or until heated through. **Yield:** 8 servings.

To use frozen hoagies: Place foil-wrapped sandwiches on a baking sheet. Bake at 375° for 60-70 minutes or until heated through.

and place in a large bowl. Cover rolls and tops with plastic wrap; set aside. To the crumbled bread, add beef, egg, milk, diced onion, salt and pepper. Shape into 27 meatballs, about 1-1/2 in. each. In a large skillet, cook meatballs over medium heat in 1 tablespoon oil for 20-25 minutes or until no longer pink. Remove with a slotted spoon; set aside.

Add remaining oil to skillet; saute green peppers and sliced onion until tender. Remove with a slotted spoon; set aside. Stir flour into skillet. Add chili sauce and water; bring to a boil. Cook and stir for 1-2 minutes. Stir in brown sugar and mustard. Add meatballs, peppers and onion; cover and simmer for 20 minutes.

Meanwhile, warm rolls in a 325° oven for 8-10 minutes. Spoon three meatballs and sauce into each roll; replace tops. **Yield:** 9 servings.

Meatball Sub Sandwiches

(Pictured above)

Kim Marie Van Rheenen, Mendota, Illinois

These hot, meaty sandwiches have a tangy barbecue-style sauce rather than the more traditional Italian tomato sauce.

    9 submarine sandwich buns
1-1/2 pounds ground beef
    1 egg
  1/4 cup milk
    1 tablespoon diced onion
    1 teaspoon salt
  1/4 teaspoon pepper
    2 tablespoons vegetable oil, *divided*
    2 medium green peppers, julienned
    1 medium onion, sliced
    1 tablespoon all-purpose flour
    1 bottle (12 ounces) chili sauce
    1 cup water
    1 tablespoon brown sugar
    1 teaspoon ground mustard

Cut a thin slice off the top of each roll; scoop out bread from inside. Crumble 1-1/4 cups of the bread

Zesty Macaroni Soup

Joan Hallford, North Richland Hills, Texas

The recipe for this thick, zippy soup first caught my attention for two reasons—it calls for ingredients that are found in my pantry, and it can be prepared in a jiffy. A chili macaroni mix provides this dish with a little spice, but sometimes I jazz it up with a can of chopped green chilies. It's a family favorite.

    1 pound ground beef
    1 medium onion, chopped
    5 cups water
    1 can (15 ounces) pinto beans, rinsed and drained
    1 can (14-1/2 ounces) diced tomatoes, undrained
    1 can (7 ounces) whole kernel corn, drained
    1 can (4 ounces) chopped green chilies, optional
  1/2 teaspoon ground mustard
  1/2 teaspoon salt
  1/8 teaspoon pepper
    1 package (7-1/2 ounces) chili macaroni dinner mix
Salsa con queso dip

In a saucepan, cook beef and onion over medium heat until meat is no longer pink; drain. Stir in water, beans, tomatoes, corn and chilies if desired. Stir in mustard, salt, pepper and contents of macaroni sauce mix. Bring to a boil. Reduce heat; cover and simmer for 10 minutes. Stir in contents of macaroni packet. Cover and simmer 10-14 minutes longer or until macaroni is tender, stirring once. Serve with salsa con queso dip. **Yield:** 8-10 servings (about 2-1/2 quarts).

Editor's Note: This recipe was tested with Hamburger Helper brand chili macaroni. Salsa con queso dip can be found in the international food section or snack aisle of most grocery stores.

Salsa Chili

(Pictured below right)

Jane Bone, Cape Coral, Florida

You'll need just five ingredients to stir up this quick-and-easy chili. We like to use medium salsa for spicier flavor, but sometimes I use half mild and half medium. Sprinkle hearty servings with shredded cheddar cheese and other tasty toppings.

  1 **pound ground beef**
  1 **medium onion, chopped**
  1 **jar (16 ounces) salsa**
  1 **can (15 ounces) pinto beans, rinsed and drained**
  1 **can (5-1/2 ounces) tomato juice**
Shredded cheddar cheese, diced peppers, sour cream and sliced green onions, optional

In a saucepan, cook beef and onion over medium heat until meat is no longer pink; drain. Stir in salsa, beans and tomato juice; heat through. If desired, garnish with cheese and peppers and serve with sour cream and onions. **Yield:** 5 servings.

Pepperoni Stromboli

Shelley Banzhaf, Maywood, Nebraska

I've made this many times when friends and family come over to watch football and basketball games. This sandwich always satisfies the huge appetites we build up cheering for our teams.

  2 **loaves (1 pound *each*) frozen bread dough, thawed**
  2 **eggs, beaten**
1/3 **cup olive oil**

1/2 **teaspoon *each* garlic powder, salt and pepper**
1/2 **teaspoon ground mustard**
1/2 **teaspoon dried oregano**
  1 **pound ground beef, cooked and drained**
  1 **package (3-1/2 ounces) sliced pepperoni**
  2 **cups (8 ounces) shredded mozzarella cheese**
  1 **cup (4 ounces) shredded cheddar cheese**
  1 **small onion, chopped**

Place each loaf of bread dough in a greased bowl, turning once to grease top. Cover and let rise in a warm place until doubled, about 45 minutes.

Punch down. Roll each loaf into a 15-in. x 12-in. rectangle. In a bowl, combine eggs, oil and seasonings. Brush over dough to within 1/2 in. of edges; set remaining egg mixture aside.

Arrange beef, pepperoni, cheeses and onion on dough to within 1/2 in. of edges. Roll up, jelly-roll style, beginning with a long side. Seal the edges well. Place seam side down on greased baking sheets. Brush with remaining egg mixture.

Bake at 375° for 30-35 minutes or until lightly browned. Let stand for 5-10 minutes before cutting. **Yield:** about 16 servings.

Double-Shell Tacos

(Pictured below)

These two-shell tacos from our Test Kitchen staff are twice the fun. A warm pita spread with refried beans enfolds a crispy taco shell filled with savory ground beef and tempting toppings.

> 1/2 pound ground beef
> 2 tablespoons taco seasoning
> 1/3 cup water
> 1/2 cup refried beans
> 2 whole gyro-style pitas (6 inches)
> 2 taco shells

Toppings: chopped green onions, chopped tomatoes, sliced ripe olives, shredded cheddar cheese, sour cream *and/or* shredded lettuce, optional

In a large skillet, cook beef over medium heat until no longer pink; drain. Stir in taco seasoning and water. Bring to a boil. Reduce heat; simmer, uncovered, for 3-4 minutes or until thickened.

Meanwhile, spread 1/4 cup refried beans over one side of each pita. Place on a microwave-safe plate; heat, uncovered, on high for 15-20 seconds or until warmed. Immediately wrap each pita around a taco shell. Fill with beef mixture. Serve with toppings of your choice. **Yield:** 2 servings.

Zesty Hominy Chili

Barbara Wheless, Sheldon, South Carolina

This robust chili is easy to prepare with canned items and receives rave reviews. The recipe makes enough for dinner with leftovers to freeze.

> 1 pound ground beef
> 1 large onion, chopped
> 2 cans (15-1/2 ounces *each*) hominy, drained
> 2 cans (14-1/2 ounces *each*) stewed tomatoes, undrained
> 1 can (15-1/4 ounces) whole kernel corn, drained
> 1 can (15 ounces) pinto beans, rinsed and drained
> 1 can (15 ounces) black beans, rinsed and drained
> 1 cup water
> 1 envelope taco seasoning
> 1 envelope ranch salad dressing mix
> 2 teaspoons ground cumin
> 1/2 teaspoon garlic salt
> 1/2 teaspoon pepper

Corn chips, optional

In a large saucepan or Dutch oven, cook beef and onion over medium heat until meat is no longer pink; drain. Stir in the next 11 ingredients.

Bring to a boil. Reduce heat; cover and simmer for 30 minutes. Serve half of the chili with corn chips if desired. Freeze remaining chili in a freezer container for up to 3 months. **Yield:** 2 batches (4-5 servings each).

To use frozen chili: Thaw in the refrigerator. Transfer to a saucepan; heat through, adding water if desired.

Beef Vegetable Soup

Carol Calhoun, Sioux Falls, South Dakota

Convenient frozen veggies and hash browns make this meaty soup a snap to mix up. Simply brown the ground beef, then stir everything together to simmer all day. It's wonderful served with bread and a salad.

> 1 pound ground beef
> 1 can (46 ounces) tomato juice
> 1 package (16 ounces) frozen mixed vegetables, thawed

> 2 cups frozen cubed hash brown
>   potatoes, thawed
> 1 envelope onion soup mix

In a large skillet, cook the beef over medium heat until no longer pink; drain. Transfer to a 5-qt. slow cooker. Stir in the tomato juice, mixed vegetables, potatoes and soup mix. Cover and cook on low for 8-9 hours or until heated through. **Yield:** 10 servings.

Barbecued Burgers

(Pictured at right and on the back cover)

Rhoda Troyer, Glenford, Ohio

I can't take all the credit for these wonderful burgers. My husband's uncle passed down the special barbecue sauce recipe we use on, and in, these burgers.

SAUCE:
>   1 cup ketchup
>   1/2 cup packed brown sugar
>   1/3 cup sugar
>   1/4 cup honey
>   1/4 cup molasses
>   2 teaspoons prepared mustard
> 1-1/2 teaspoons Worcestershire sauce
>   1/4 teaspoon salt
>   1/4 teaspoon Liquid Smoke
>   1/8 teaspoon pepper

BURGERS:
>   1 egg, beaten
>   1/3 cup quick-cooking oats
>   1/4 teaspoon onion salt
>   1/4 teaspoon garlic salt
>   1/4 teaspoon pepper
>   1/8 teaspoon salt
> 1-1/2 pounds ground beef
>   6 hamburger buns, split

Toppings of your choice

In a small saucepan, combine the first 10 ingredients. Bring to a boil. Remove from the heat. Set aside 1 cup barbecue sauce to serve with burgers.

In a bowl, combine the egg, oats, 1/4 cup of the remaining barbecue sauce, onion salt, garlic salt, pepper and salt. Crumble beef over mixture; mix well. Shape into six patties.

Grill, covered, over medium heat for 6-8 minutes on each side or until a meat thermometer reads 160°, basting with 1/2 cup barbecue sauce during the last 5 minutes. Serve on buns with

toppings of your choice and reserved barbecue sauce. **Yield:** 6 servings.

Taco Pasta Salad

Gert Rosenau, Pewaukee, Wisconsin

I blend the best of two popular salads into one satisfying main dish. Serve taco or corn chips on the side, and you have a complete meal.

>   2 cups uncooked spiral pasta
>   1 pound ground beef
>   1 envelope taco seasoning
>   3 cups shredded lettuce
>   2 cups halved cherry tomatoes
>   1 cup (4 ounces) shredded cheddar cheese
> 1/2 cup chopped onion
> 1/2 cup chopped green pepper
> 1/2 cup Catalina salad dressing

Tortilla chips

Cook pasta according to package directions. Meanwhile, in a skillet, cook beef over medium heat until no longer pink; drain. Stir in the taco seasoning; cool.

Drain pasta and rinse in cold water; stir into meat mixture. Add the lettuce, tomatoes, cheese, onion, green pepper and dressing; toss to coat. Serve with tortilla chips. **Yield:** 6 servings.

Pizzas, Pies
& Pockets

Chapter 3

while, cook beef and onion in a skillet over medium heat until meat is no longer pink; drain.

Punch dough down; divide in half. Press into two greased 12-in. pizza pans. Combine tomato sauce, oregano and basil; spread over each crust. Top with beef mixture, green pepper and cheese. Bake at 400° for 25-30 minutes or until crust is lightly browned. **Yield:** 2 pizzas (6 servings).

Upper Peninsula Pasties

Carole Lynn Derifield, Valdez, Alaska

I grew up in Michigan's Upper Peninsula, where many people are of English ancestry and where pasties—traditional meat pies often eaten by hand—are popular.

      2 **cups shortening**
      2 **cups boiling water**
5-1/2 to 6 **cups all-purpose flour**
      2 **teaspoons salt**
FILLING:
     12 **large red potatoes (about 6 pounds), peeled**
      4 **medium rutabagas (about 3 pounds), peeled**
      2 **medium onions, chopped**
      2 **pounds ground beef**
      1 **pound ground pork**
      1 **tablespoon salt**
      2 **teaspoons pepper**
      2 **teaspoons garlic powder**
    1/4 **cup butter**
Half-and-half cream, optional

In a large bowl, stir shortening and water until shortening is melted. Gradually stir in flour and salt until a very soft dough is formed; cover and refrigerate for 1-1/2 hours.

Quarter and thinly slice potatoes and rutabagas; place in a large bowl with onions, beef, pork and seasonings. Divide dough into 12 equal portions. On a floured surface, roll out one portion at a time into a 10-in. circle. Mound about 2 cups filling on half of each circle; dot with 1 teaspoon butter. Moisten edges with water; fold dough over filling and press edges with a fork to seal. Place on ungreased baking sheets. Cut several slits in top of pasties. Brush with cream if desired.

Bake at 350° for 1 hour or until golden brown. Cool on wire racks. Serve hot or cold. Store in the refrigerator. **Yield:** 12 servings.

Homemade Pizza

(Pictured above)

Marianne Edwards, Lake Stevens, Washington

Homemade Pizza is a hearty, zesty main dish with a crisp, golden crust.

      1 **package (1/4 ounce) active dry yeast**
      1 **teaspoon sugar**
  1-1/4 **cups warm water (110° to 115°)**
    1/4 **cup vegetable oil**
      1 **teaspoon salt**
  3-1/2 **cups all-purpose flour**
    1/2 **pound ground beef**
      1 **small onion, chopped**
      1 **can (15 ounces) tomato sauce**
      1 **tablespoon dried oregano**
      1 **teaspoon dried basil**
      1 **medium green pepper, diced**
      2 **cups (8 ounces) shredded mozzarella cheese**

In large bowl, dissolve yeast and sugar in water; let stand for 5 minutes. Add oil and salt. Stir in flour, 1 cup at a time, to form soft dough. Turn onto a floured surface; knead until smooth and elastic, about 2-3 minutes. Place in a greased bowl, turning once to grease top. Cover and let rise in a warm place until doubled, about 45 minutes. Mean-

Finnish Meat Pie

Laurel Skoog, Frazee, Minnesota

We enjoy this traditional meat pie year-round, but it's especially appreciated during hunting season. This is one recipe I'll be sure to pass on to our seven children.

  1 **cup water**
  1 **teaspoon salt**
  1 **cup shortening**
  3 **cups all-purpose flour**
FILLING:
  4 **cups shredded peeled potatoes**
1-1/2 **pounds ground beef**
  2 **cups shredded carrots**
  1 **medium onion, chopped**
1/2 **cup shredded peeled rutabaga**
1-1/2 **teaspoons salt**
1/4 **teaspoon pepper**

In a saucepan, combine water and salt; bring to a boil. Remove from the heat. Stir in shortening until melted. Add flour; stir until a soft ball forms. Cover and refrigerate until cool, about 1 hour.

Divide dough in half. On a floured surface, roll one portion of dough to fit the bottom of a 13-in. x 9-in. x 2-in. baking dish. Line ungreased dish with pastry.

In a bowl, combine filling ingredients; mix well. Spoon into crust. Roll out remaining pastry to fit top of dish. Place over filling; press edges with a fork to seal. Cut slits in top. Bake at 350° for 1-1/4 hours or until golden brown. **Yield:** 6-8 servings.

Peppery Pizza Loaves

(Pictured below)

Lou Stasny, Poplarville, Mississippi

I often take these French bread pizzas to church picnics or potluck suppers, and there is never any left. When I fix them for the two of us, I freeze two halves in foil.

1-1/2 **pounds ground beef**
  1/2 **teaspoon garlic powder**
  1/2 **teaspoon salt**
    2 **loaves (8 ounces *each*) French bread, halved lengthwise**
    1 **jar (8 ounces) process cheese sauce**
    1 **can (4 ounces) mushroom stems and pieces, drained**
    1 **cup chopped green onions**
    1 **can (4 ounces) sliced jalapenos, drained**
    1 **can (8 ounces) tomato sauce**
  1/2 **cup grated Parmesan cheese**
    4 **cups (16 ounces) shredded mozzarella cheese**

In a skillet, cook beef over medium heat until no longer pink; drain. Stir in garlic powder and salt. Place each bread half on a large piece of heavy-duty foil. Spread with cheese sauce. Top with beef mixture, mushrooms, onions and jalapenos. Drizzle with tomato sauce. Top with Parmesan and mozzarella cheeses. Wrap and freeze. May be frozen for up to 3 months. **Yield:** 4 loaves (2-3 servings each).

To bake: Unwrap loaves and thaw on baking sheets in the refrigerator. Bake at 350° for 18 minutes or until cheese is melted.

Hash Brown Beef Pie

(Pictured below)

Mina Dyck, Boissevain, Manitoba

Convenient frozen hash browns and shredded cheddar cheese top this hearty mixture of vegetables and ground beef. It has just the right combination of spices. Because I'm cooking for one, I like that the leftovers reheat well in the microwave.

- 1 **pound ground beef**
- 1 **medium onion, chopped**
- 1 **garlic clove, minced**
- 1 **can (14-1/2 ounces) diced tomatoes, drained**
- 1 **teaspoon chili powder**
- 1 **teaspoon dried oregano**
- 1/2 **teaspoon salt**
- 1/4 **teaspoon pepper**
- 1-1/2 **cups frozen mixed vegetables**

TOPPING:

- 3 **cups frozen shredded hash brown potatoes, thawed and drained**
- 1 **cup (8 ounces) shredded cheddar cheese**
- 1 **egg**
- 1/8 **teaspoon salt**
- 1/8 **teaspoon pepper**

In a large skillet, cook beef, onion and garlic over medium heat until beef is no longer pink; drain. Stir in tomatoes, chili powder, oregano, salt and pepper; bring to a boil. Reduce heat; simmer, uncovered, for 10 minutes. Stir in the vegetables.

Pour into a greased 9-in. pie plate. Combine topping ingredients; spoon evenly over the meat mixture. Bake, uncovered, at 400° for 30 minutes. **Yield:** 6-8 servings.

Nutty Beef Turnovers

Jim McLean, Roseau, Minnesota

With crunchy nuts and a touch of cinnamon, these turnovers tantalize taste buds.

- 1 **pound ground beef**
- 1-1/2 **cups chopped nuts**
- 1 **medium onion, chopped**
- 2 **garlic cloves, minced**
- 1 **tablespoon Worcestershire sauce**
- 2 **teaspoons sugar**
- 1/4 **teaspoon ground cinnamon**
- 2 **loaves (1 pound *each*) frozen bread dough, thawed**

In a skillet, cook beef, nuts, onion and garlic over medium heat until meat is no longer pink; drain. Remove from the heat. Stir in the Worcestershire sauce, sugar and cinnamon.

On a floured surface, roll each portion of dough into a 12-in. square. Cut each into four squares. Place about 1/4 cup meat mixture in center of each square. Moisten edges of pastry with water; fold over filling, forming a triangle. Press edges with a fork to seal. Place on ungreased baking sheets. Bake at 350° for 20 minutes or until golden brown. **Yield:** 8 servings.

Personal Pizzas

Julie Beth Lamb, Visalia, California

I practically lived on these mini pizzas when I was in college. Packaged pizza crust mixes make it an easy recipe.

- 2 **packages (6-1/2 ounces *each*) pizza crust mix**
- 1-1/2 **cups pizza sauce**

1 pound ground beef, cooked and drained
1 medium onion, chopped
1 cup chopped green pepper
2 cans (2-1/4 ounces *each*) sliced ripe
    olives, drained
2 cups (8 ounces) shredded mozzarella
    cheese

Prepare both packages of pizza dough according to directions. On a floured surface, knead dough several times; divide into six portions. Roll each into an 8-in. circle. Place on greased baking sheets. Bake at 425° for 10 minutes.

Spread pizza sauce over crusts to within 1/2 in. of edge. Top with beef, onion, green pepper, olives and cheese. Return to the oven for 10-15 minutes or until crust is golden brown and cheese is melted. **Yield:** 6 servings.

Mushroom Burger Pockets

Rose Sadowsky, Dickinson, North Dakota

These hearty hand-held pockets are favored by my husband and sons.

1-1/2 pounds ground beef
    1 can (10-3/4 ounces) condensed cream
        of mushroom soup, undiluted
    1 can (4 ounces) mushroom stems and
        pieces, drained
    1 medium onion, chopped
    1 tablespoon Worcestershire sauce
Salt and pepper to taste
    1 loaf (1 pound) frozen bread dough,
        thawed
    1 cup (4 ounces) shredded cheddar
        cheese

In a skillet, cook beef over medium heat until no longer pink; drain. Stir in the soup, mushrooms, onion, Worcestershire sauce, salt and pepper. Remove from the heat.

On a floured surface, roll dough into a 16-in. x 8-in. rectangle. Cut into eight squares. Place about 1/3 cup meat mixture in the center of each square; sprinkle with cheese. Bring the four corners to center over filling; pinch seams together to seal.

Place seam side down on greased baking sheets. Cover and let rise in a warm place for 15-20 minutes. Bake at 350° for 20-25 minutes or until golden brown. **Yield:** 8 servings.

Meat Shell Potato Pie

(Pictured above)

Julie Sterchi, Flora, Illinois

Guests always comment on the unique presentation and flavor of this delightfully different dish.

    1 pound ground beef
    1 can (10-3/4 ounces) condensed cream
        of mushroom soup, undiluted, *divided*
1/4 cup chopped onion
    1 egg
1/4 cup dry bread crumbs
    2 tablespoons chopped fresh parsley
1/4 teaspoon salt
Pinch pepper
    2 cups mashed potatoes
    4 bacon strips, cooked and crumbled
1/2 cup shredded cheddar cheese

In a large bowl, combine beef, 1/2 cup soup, onion, egg, bread crumbs, parsley, salt and pepper; mix well. Press onto the bottom and up the sides of a 9-in. pie plate. Bake at 350° for 25 minutes; drain.

Combine potatoes and remaining soup in a bowl; mix until fluffy. Spread over meat crust. Sprinkle with bacon and cheese. Bake at 350° for 15 minutes. Let stand for a few minutes. Cut into wedges. **Yield:** 6 servings.

pink; drain and set aside. In a saucepan, bring the tomato sauce and Italian seasoning to a boil. Reduce heat; cover and simmer for 5 minutes. Stir 1/2 cup sauce into the meat mixture; keep the remaining sauce warm.

Unroll pizza crust on a floured surface. Roll into a 12-in. square; cut into four squares. Spread cream cheese over each to within 1/2 in. of edges. Top with meat mixture. Sprinkle with mozzarella cheese, mushrooms and olives.

Fold dough over the filling, forming a triangle; press the edges with a fork to seal. Place on a greased baking sheet.

Bake at 400° for 20-25 minutes or until golden brown. Serve the calzones with the remaining sauce. **Yield:** 4 servings.

Super Calzones

(Pictured above)

Laronda Warrick, Parker, Kansas

A friend gave this recipe to me at my wedding shower years ago. I realized then and there that I'd better learn how to make them! My husband loves these hand-held calzones.

　1/2　pound ground beef
　　2　tablespoons finely chopped onion
　　2　tablespoons finely chopped green
　　　　pepper
　　1　garlic clove, minced
　　1　can (15 ounces) tomato sauce
　　1　teaspoon Italian seasoning
　　1　tube (10 ounces) refrigerated pizza
　　　　crust
　　1　package (3 ounces) cream cheese,
　　　　softened
　　1　cup (4 ounces) shredded mozzarella
　　　　cheese
　　1　can (4 ounces) mushroom stems and
　　　　pieces, drained
　　1　can (2-1/4 ounces) sliced ripe olives,
　　　　drained

In a skillet, cook the beef, onion, green pepper and garlic over medium heat until meat is no longer

Herbed Pasties

Jean Kitchen, Monroe, Oregon

My husband likes to eat whatever I cook, but he really looks forward to these herbed meat pies. We eat them as sandwiches or on a plate smothered with from-scratch brown gravy.

1-1/2　pounds ground beef
　　1　medium onion, chopped
　　2　beef bouillon cubes
　1/4　cup boiling water
1-1/2　cups (6 ounces) shredded cheddar
　　　　cheese
　　1　cup sliced fresh mushrooms
　　1　celery rib, diced
　1/4　cup grated Parmesan cheese
　3/4　teaspoon dill weed
　3/4　teaspoon dried thyme
　1/2　teaspoon dried rosemary, crushed
Salt and pepper to taste
　　2　packages (11 ounces *each*) pie crust mix
　　1　egg
　　1　tablespoon water

In a skillet, cook the beef and onion over medium heat until the meat is no longer pink; drain well. Dissolve the bouillon in water; stir into meat mixture. Add the cheddar cheese, mushrooms, celery, Parmesan cheese, dill weed, thyme, rosemary, salt and pepper; mix well.

Prepare pie crusts according to package directions. Divide dough into four portions. On a floured surface, roll each into a 14-in. square. Cut each into four 7-in. squares.

Place a scant 1/2 cup meat mixture in the center of each square. Moisten edges of pastry with water and fold over filling, forming a triangle. Press edges with a fork to seal. Make a 1-in. slit in the top of each triangle. Place on two ungreased baking sheets.

Beat egg and water; brush over pastry. Bake at 375° for 30-35 minutes or until golden brown. **Yield:** 16 servings.

Ground Beef 'n' Rice Pie

Rhonda Van Gelderen
Menomonee Falls, Wisconsin

I press seasoned ground beef into a pie plate to form the crust of this comforting dish. It's a terrific time-saver, especially on hectic days, because you don't brown the beef separately.

- 1 **pound uncooked ground beef**
- 1 **can (15 ounces) tomato sauce,** *divided*
- 1/2 **cup dry bread crumbs**
- 1/4 **cup chopped onion**
- 1/4 **cup chopped green pepper,** **optional**
- 1/2 **teaspoon salt**
- 1/2 **teaspoon Italian seasoning**
- 1/8 **teaspoon dried oregano**
- 1/8 **teaspoon pepper**
- 1 **can (6 ounces) tomato paste**
- 2-1/2 **cups cooked rice**
- 1 **cup (4 ounces) shredded cheddar** **cheese,** *divided*

In a bowl, combine beef, 3/4 cup tomato sauce, bread crumbs, onion, green pepper if desired and seasonings. Press evenly onto the bottom and up the sides of an ungreased 9-in. pie plate, forming a crust.

In a bowl, combine the tomato paste and remaining tomato sauce. Stir in the rice and 3/4 cup cheese; pour into crust. Place pie plate on a baking sheet. Cover and bake at 350° for 25 minutes or until the meat is no longer pink.

Uncover; drain. Sprinkle with remaining cheese. Bake 10-15 minutes longer or until the cheese is melted. Let stand for 5 minutes before cutting. **Yield:** 6-8 servings.

Cheeseburger Pockets

(Pictured below)

Pat Chambless, Crowder, Oklahoma

Ground beef is my favorite meat to cook with because it's so versatile, flavorful and economical. Refrigerated biscuits save you the trouble of making dough from scratch.

- 1/2 **pound ground beef**
- 1 **tablespoon chopped onion**
- 1/2 **teaspoon salt**
- 1/8 **teaspoon pepper**
- 1 **tube (12 ounces) refrigerated buttermilk** **biscuits**
- 5 **slices process American cheese**

In a skillet, cook beef, onion, salt and pepper over medium heat until meat is no longer pink; drain and cool. Place two biscuits overlapping on a floured surface; roll out into a 5-in. oval. Place 3 tablespoons meat mixture on one side. Fold a cheese slice to fit over meat mixture. Fold dough over filling; press edges with a fork to seal.

Repeat with remaining biscuits, meat mixture and cheese. Place on a greased baking sheet. Prick tops with a fork. Bake at 400° for 10 minutes or until golden brown. **Yield:** 5 servings.

Deep-Dish Pizza

(Pictured below)

Patricia Howson, Carstairs, Alberta

My family devours this crusty pan pizza with delicious toppings. Use a combination of green, red and yellow peppers for added color.

    1 package (1/4 ounce) active dry yeast
    1 cup warm water (110° to 115°)
    1 teaspoon sugar
    1 teaspoon salt
    2 tablespoons vegetable oil
2-1/2 cups all-purpose flour
    1 pound ground beef, cooked and drained
    1 can (10-3/4 ounces) condensed tomato
      soup, undiluted
    1 teaspoon *each* dried basil, oregano and
      thyme
    1 teaspoon dried rosemary, crushed
  1/4 teaspoon garlic powder
    1 small green pepper, julienned
    1 can (8 ounces) mushroom stems and
      pieces, drained
    1 cup (4 ounces) shredded mozzarella
      cheese

In a bowl, dissolve yeast in water. Stir in sugar, salt, oil and flour. Beat vigorously 20 strokes. Cover and let rest for 20 minutes. On a floured surface, roll into a 13-in. x 9-in. rectangle. Transfer to a greased 13-in. x 9-in. x 2-in. baking pan. Sprinkle with beef.

Combine soup and seasonings; spoon over beef. Top with green pepper, mushrooms and cheese. Bake at 425° for 20-25 minutes or until crust and cheese are lightly browned. **Yield:** 8 servings.

Savory Triangles

Holly Massie, Pearce, Arizona

I learned to cook by watching my mom and helping when I could. She still teaches me by sharing tried-and-true recipes like this.

    1 pound ground beef
    1 large tomato, seeded and chopped
  1/2 cup thinly sliced green onions
    1 garlic clove, minced
  1/2 teaspoon salt
  1/2 teaspoon crushed red pepper flakes
  1/2 teaspoon dried thyme
    2 teaspoons cornstarch
  2/3 cup beef broth
Pastry for double-crust pie (9 inches)
    1 egg, beaten

In a skillet, cook beef, tomato, onions and garlic over medium heat until meat is no longer pink; drain. Stir in salt, red pepper flakes and thyme. In a small bowl, combine cornstarch and broth until smooth. Add to meat mixture. Bring to a boil; cook and stir for 2 minutes or until thickened. Remove from the heat.

On a floured surface, roll the pastry into two 12-in. squares. Cut each into four squares. Spoon about 1/4 cup meat mixture in the center of each square. Moisten edges of pastry with egg; fold over filling, forming a triangle. Press the edges with a fork to seal.

Place on ungreased baking sheets; prick tops with a fork. Bake at 425° for 10-15 minutes or until golden brown. **Yield:** 8 servings.

Speedy Beef Pasties

Jeannine Ellis, Michigan City, Indiana

I find it very convenient to make these pasties ahead of time and freeze. That way I can thaw and bake just the right amount needed for the two of us.

1 pound ground beef
1/4 cup chopped onion
1 can (8 ounces) diced carrots, drained
1 medium potato, peeled and shredded
1 cup (4 ounces) shredded cheddar
   cheese
1/4 cup ketchup
1 tablespoon prepared mustard
1/2 teaspoon garlic salt
1/4 teaspoon pepper
2 packages (11 ounces *each*) pie crust mix

In a skillet, cook beef and onion over medium heat until meat is no longer pink; drain. Remove from the heat. Stir in carrots, potato, cheese, ketchup, mustard, garlic salt and pepper. Prepare pie crusts according to package directions.

On a floured surface, roll each portion into a 12-in. square. Cut each into four squares. Place about 1/2 cup meat mixture in the center of each square. Moisten edges of pastry with water and fold over filling, forming a triangle. Press edges with a fork to seal; prick tops with a fork.

Place on ungreased baking sheets. Bake at 375° for 30 minutes or until golden brown. **Yield:** 8 servings.

Spicy Shepherd's Pie

(Pictured above right)

Mary and Wayne Malchow, Neenah, Wisconsin

This hearty main dish is a zestier version of a recipe I found in a cookbook. I top it off with instant mashed potatoes, which are quick to stir up while I cook the beef.

1 package (6.6 ounces) instant mashed
   potatoes
1 pound ground beef
1 medium onion, chopped
1 can (14-1/2 ounces) diced tomatoes,
   undrained
1 can (11 ounces) Mexicorn, drained
1 can (2-1/4 ounces) sliced ripe olives,
   drained
1 envelope taco seasoning
1-1/2 teaspoons chili powder
1/2 teaspoon salt
1/8 teaspoon garlic powder
1 cup (4 ounces) shredded cheddar
   cheese, *divided*

Prepare mashed potatoes according to package directions. Meanwhile, in a large skillet, cook beef and onion over medium heat until the meat is no longer pink; drain. Add tomatoes, corn, olives, taco seasoning, chili powder, salt and garlic powder. Bring to a boil; cook and stir for 1-2 minutes.

Transfer to a greased 2-1/2-qt. baking dish. Top with 3/4 cup cheese. Spread mashed potatoes over the top; sprinkle with remaining cheese. Bake, uncovered, at 350° for 12-15 minutes or until cheese is melted. **Yield:** 4-6 servings.

Editor's Note: 4-1/2 cups hot mashed potatoes (prepared with milk and butter) may be substituted for the instant mashed potatoes.

Pizza Particulars

To prevent a homemade pizza crust from getting soggy, lightly saute vegetables with a high water content, like mushrooms, bell peppers and onions, before using them as toppings.

For the crispest crust, try putting a thin layer of cheese under the sauce and toppings, then top with more cheese if desired. The bottom cheese layer provides a buffer between the crust and moist toppings.

Tasty Meat Pies

(Pictured above and on cover)

Cheryl Cattane, Lapeer, Michigan

I work full time as a nurse, so I like meals that are quick and easy. This comforting all-in-one pie is filled with ground beef and tender vegetables.

    1 pound ground beef
    1 small onion, chopped
    1 can (11 ounces) condensed beef with
       vegetables and barley soup, undiluted
    1 can (10-3/4 ounces) condensed golden
       mushroom soup, undiluted
    3 medium uncooked potatoes, cut
       into 1/2-inch cubes
    4 medium carrots, sliced 1/8 inch thick
  1/4 teaspoon salt
  1/8 teaspoon pepper
Pastry for double-crust pie (9 inches)

In a skillet, cook beef and onion over medium heat until meat is no longer pink; drain. Add the soups, potatoes, carrots, salt and pepper; mix well. Divide between two ungreased 9-in. pie plates.

On a floured surface, roll pastry to fit top of each pie; place over filling. Seal and flute edges; cut slits in top. Bake at 350° for 45-50 minutes or until golden brown. Let stand on a wire rack for 15 minutes before serving. **Yield:** 2 pies (6 servings each).

Taco Puffs

Jan Schmid, Hibbing, Minnesota

I got this recipe from a friend years ago and still make these cheesy sandwiches regularly. I serve them for dinner with a steaming bowl of soup or fresh salad.

    1 pound ground beef
  1/2 cup chopped onion
    1 envelope taco seasoning
    2 tubes (17.3 ounces each) large
       refrigerated biscuits
    8 ounces cheddar cheese, cut into 16
       slices or 2 cups (8 ounces) shredded
       cheddar cheese

In a skillet, cook beef and onion over medium heat until meat is no longer pink and onion is tender; drain. Add the taco seasoning and prepare according to package directions. Cool slightly.

Flatten half of the biscuits into 4-in. circles; place in greased 15-in. x 10-in. x 1-in. baking pans. Spoon 1/4 cup meat mixture onto each; top with two cheese slices or 1/4 cup shredded cheese. Flatten the remaining biscuits; place on top and pinch edges to seal tightly. Bake at 400° for 15 minutes or until golden brown. **Yield:** 5 servings.

Upside-Down Pizza

Karen Cook, Putnam Station, New York

When everyone craves pizza and you have no refrigerated dough on hand and no time to prepare a homemade crust, try this upside-down version.

    1 pound ground beef
    1 medium onion, chopped
    1 jar (14 ounces) spaghetti sauce
    2 cups (8 ounces) shredded mozzarella
       cheese
    1 cup milk
    2 eggs
    1 teaspoon vegetable oil
    1 cup all-purpose flour
  1/2 teaspoon salt

In a large skillet, cook beef and onion over medium heat until the meat is no longer pink; drain. Add spaghetti sauce. Cover and simmer until heated through. Pour into a greased 13-in. x 9-in. x 2-in. baking dish. Sprinkle with cheese.

In a blender, combine the milk, eggs, oil, flour and salt; cover and process until smooth. Pour over cheese. Bake, uncovered, at 400° for 25-30 minutes or until golden brown. **Yield:** 12 servings.

Bean 'n' Beef Crescent Pie

Marla Miller, Englewood, Tennessee

My husband loves this meal. Convenient crescent roll dough is the speedy crust for this savory south-of-the-border sensation.

1-1/4   pounds ground beef
   1   envelope taco seasoning
 1/3   cup salsa
   1   tube (8 ounces) refrigerated crescent rolls
   4   ounces cream cheese, softened
 1/2   cup refried beans
   1   cup (4 ounces) shredded Mexican cheese blend

In a large skillet, cook the beef over medium heat until no longer pink; drain. Add taco seasoning and salsa; simmer, uncovered, until thickened. Meanwhile, unroll crescent roll dough. Press onto the bottom and up the sides of an ungreased 13-in. x 9-in. x 2-in. baking dish; seal perforations. Spread cream cheese over the dough.

Stir the refried beans into beef mixture. Spoon over cream cheese layer. Bake, uncovered, at 375° for 20-25 minutes or until crust is golden brown. Sprinkle with cheese; bake 5 minutes longer or until the cheese is melted. **Yield:** 6-8 servings.

Spinach-Beef Spaghetti Pie

(Pictured at right)

Carol Hicks, Pensacola, Florida

With its angel hair pasta crust, this cheesy ground beef, tomato and spinach pie is always a hit when I serve it. Each neat slice has layers of pasta, cream cheese filling and spinach topping.

   6   ounces uncooked angel hair pasta
   2   eggs, lightly beaten
 1/3   cup grated Parmesan cheese
   1   pound ground beef
 1/2   cup chopped onion
 1/4   cup chopped green pepper
   1   jar (14 ounces) meatless spaghetti sauce
   1   teaspoon Creole seasoning
 3/4   teaspoon garlic powder
 1/2   teaspoon dried basil
 1/2   teaspoon dried oregano
   1   package (8 ounces) cream cheese, softened
   1   package (10 ounces) frozen chopped spinach, thawed and squeezed dry
 1/2   cup shredded mozzarella cheese

Cook pasta according to package directions; drain. Add eggs and Parmesan cheese. Press onto the bottom and up the sides of a greased 9-in. deep-dish pie plate. Bake at 350° for 10 minutes.

Meanwhile, in a skillet, cook the beef, onion and green pepper over medium heat until meat is no longer pink; drain. Stir in spaghetti sauce and seasonings. Bring to a boil. Reduce heat; cover and simmer for 10 minutes.

Between two pieces of waxed paper, roll out cream cheese into a 7-in. circle. Place in the crust. Top with spinach and meat sauce. Sprinkle with mozzarella cheese. Bake at 350° for 20-30 minutes or until set. **Yield:** 6-8 servings.

Corn Tortilla Pizzas

(Pictured below and on page 34)

Karen Housley-Raatz, Walworth, Wisconsin

These tasty individual pizzas have the zippy flavor of tacos. When I created this recipe and served these pizzas to my husband and day-care kids, they made them disappear. The recipe produces a big batch of the meat mixture, but leftovers can be frozen for up to 3 months.

1-1/4	pounds ground beef
1	small onion, chopped
1/2	cup chopped green pepper
3	cans (6 ounces *each*) tomato paste
1-1/4	cups water
1	cup salsa
2	cups fresh *or* frozen corn
1-1/2	cups chopped fresh tomatoes
3/4	cup chopped ripe olives
1	envelope taco seasoning
3	teaspoons garlic powder
1-1/2	teaspoons dried parsley flakes
1/2	teaspoon dried oregano
1/8	teaspoon salt
1/4	teaspoon pepper
32	corn *or* flour tortillas (6 inches)
8	cups (2 pounds) shredded mozzarella cheese

In a skillet, cook beef, onion and green pepper over medium heat until meat is no longer pink; drain. In a bowl, combine tomato paste and water until blended; add salsa. Stir into meat mixture. Stir in corn, tomatoes, olives and seasonings.

Place tortillas on ungreased baking sheets. Spread each with 1/4 cup meat mixture to within 1/2 in. of edge and sprinkle with 1/4 cup of cheese. Bake at 375° for 5-7 minutes or until the cheese is melted. **Yield:** 32 pizzas.

Beef Turnovers

Judie Sadighi, Twain Harte, California

My husband and I developed this recipe for the restaurant we own and operate. We make a limited number each day and never have a problem selling out.

2	pounds ground beef
1/2	teaspoon salt
1/4	teaspoon pepper
1	can (4 ounces) mushroom stems and pieces, drained
1/3	cup chopped green onions
1/4	cup minced fresh parsley
2	tablespoons butter
2	medium tomatoes, diced
1	can (2-1/4 ounces) sliced ripe olives, drained
1/4	cup grated Parmesan cheese

DOUGH:

4	cups all-purpose flour
4	teaspoons baking powder
1	teaspoon baking soda
1/2	teaspoon salt
1/2	cup shortening
1-1/2	cups milk

Spaghetti sauce, warmed
Shredded mozzarella cheese and additional Parmesan cheese, optional

In a skillet, cook beef over medium heat until no longer pink; drain. Add salt and pepper; remove and set aside. In the same skillet, saute mushrooms, onions and parsley in butter until tender. Add tomatoes; simmer for 5 minutes. Add the olives, Parmesan cheese and beef; mix well. Cool.

In a large bowl, combine flour, baking powder, baking soda and salt. Cut in shortening until mixture resembles coarse crumbs. Stir in milk. Turn onto a floured surface; knead 10 times. Divide dough into eight portions. Roll each into an 8-in. circle. Place on greased baking sheets. Mound about 1/2 cup filling on half of each circle. Fold dough over filling and press edges with a fork to seal. Bake at 375° for 30 minutes or until golden brown. Top with spaghetti sauce and cheeses if desired. **Yield:** 8 servings.

Spicy Bean and Beef Pie

Debra Dohy, Massillon, Ohio

My daughter helped me come up with this recipe when we wanted a one-dish meal that was different from a casserole. This pie slices nicely and is a fun and filling dish.

- 1 pound ground beef
- 2 to 3 garlic cloves, minced
- 1 can (11-1/2 ounces) condensed bean with bacon soup, undiluted
- 1 jar (16 ounces) thick and chunky picante sauce, *divided*
- 1/4 cup cornstarch
- 1 tablespoon chopped fresh parsley
- 1 teaspoon paprika
- 1 teaspoon salt
- 1/4 teaspoon pepper
- 1 can (16 ounces) kidney beans, rinsed and drained
- 1 can (15 ounces) black beans, rinsed and drained
- 2 cups (8 ounces) shredded cheddar cheese, *divided*
- 3/4 cup sliced green onions, *divided*
- Pastry for double-crust pie (10 inches)
- 1 cup (8 ounces) sour cream
- 1 can (2-1/4 ounces) sliced ripe olives, drained

In a skillet, cook beef and garlic over medium heat until meat is no longer pink; drain. In a large bowl, combine soup, 1 cup picante sauce, cornstarch, parsley, paprika, salt and pepper; mix well. Fold in beans, 1-1/4 cups cheese, 1/2 cup onions and the beef mixture.

Line pie plate with bottom pastry; fill with bean mixture. Top with remaining pastry; seal and flute edges. Cut slits in the top crust. Bake at 425° for 30-35 minutes or until lightly browned. Let stand for 5 minutes before cutting. Garnish with sour cream, olives and remaining picante sauce, cheese and onions. **Yield:** 8 servings.

Bacon Cheeseburger Pizza

(Pictured above)

Cherie Ackerman, Lakeland, Minnesota

Kids of all ages love pizza and cheeseburgers...and this recipe combines them both. My grandchildren usually request pizza for supper when they visit me. They like to help me assemble this version—and they especially enjoy eating it!

- 1/2 pound ground beef
- 1 small onion, chopped
- 1 prebaked Italian bread shell crust (1 pound)
- 1 can (8 ounces) pizza sauce
- 6 bacon strips, cooked and crumbled
- 20 dill pickle coin slices
- 2 cups (8 ounces) shredded mozzarella cheese
- 2 cups (8 ounces) shredded cheddar cheese
- 1 teaspoon pizza *or* Italian seasoning

In a skillet, cook beef and onion over medium heat until meat is no longer pink; drain and set aside. Place crust on an ungreased 12-in. pizza pan. Spread with pizza sauce. Top with beef mixture, bacon, pickles and cheeses. Sprinkle with pizza seasoning. Bake at 450° for 8-10 minutes or until cheese is melted. **Yield:** 8 slices.

Beef and Tomato Pie

June Mullins, Livonia, Missouri

I bake this hot and hearty ground beef pie when my grandchildren come to visit. They like its family-pleasing flavor.

- 1 pound ground beef
- 1 large onion, chopped
- 2 tablespoons ketchup
- 1/2 teaspoon salt
- 2 cups biscuit/baking mix
- 2/3 cup milk
- 1 cup diced fresh tomato
- 1/2 cup shredded cheddar cheese

In a skillet, cook beef and onion over medium heat until meat is no longer pink; drain. Remove from the heat. Stir in ketchup and salt; set aside.

Combine biscuit mix and milk just until moistened. Turn onto a lightly floured surface and knead 6-8 times. Roll into a 10-in. circle; transfer to a greased 9-in. pie plate. Flute edges. Spoon meat mixture into crust. Sprinkle with tomatoes.

Bake at 425° for 20-25 minutes. Sprinkle with cheese; bake 2 minutes longer or until cheese is melted. **Yield:** 6 servings.

Bubble Pizza

(Pictured above)

Jo Groth, Plainfield, Iowa

A top-ranked food with teens, pizza can quickly quell a growling tummy! This recipe has a no-fuss crust made from refrigerated biscuits. For a jazzed-up version, add all of your favorite toppings.

- 1-1/2 pounds ground beef
- 1 can (15 ounces) pizza sauce
- 2 tubes (12 ounces *each*) refrigerated buttermilk biscuits
- 1-1/2 cups (6 ounces) shredded mozzarella cheese
- 1 cup (4 ounces) shredded cheddar cheese

In a skillet, cook the beef over medium heat until no longer pink; drain. Stir in pizza sauce. Quarter the biscuits; place in a greased 13-in. x 9-in. x 2-in. baking dish. Top with the beef mixture.

Bake, uncovered, at 400° for 20-25 minutes. Sprinkle with cheeses. Bake 5-10 minutes longer or until cheese is melted. Let stand for 5-10 minutes before serving. **Yield:** 6-8 servings.

Beefy Hash Brown Pizza

Betty Warren, Maryville, Tennessee

Hash brown potatoes form the crust for this fun pizza variation. When my children were growing up, this dish became a favorite Friday night treat. Now my grandchildren ask for it every time they spend a Friday night with us.

- 5 cups frozen shredded hash brown potatoes, thawed
- 1 can (10-3/4 ounces) cheddar cheese soup, undiluted
- 1 egg, lightly beaten
- 1/2 teaspoon salt
- 1/4 teaspoon pepper
- 2 pounds ground beef
- 1 medium onion, chopped
- 1 can (4 ounces) mushroom stems and pieces, drained
- 1 can (15 ounces) pizza sauce
- 4 cups (16 ounces) shredded Italian-blend cheese, *divided*

In a bowl, combine the potatoes, soup, egg, salt and pepper. Spread mixture into a greased 15-in. x 10-in. x 1-in. baking pan. Bake at 400° for 20-25 minutes or until lightly browned.

Meanwhile, in a large skillet, cook the beef, onion and mushrooms over medium heat until the meat is no longer pink; drain. Stir in pizza sauce; keep warm.

Sprinkle 2 cups cheese over hot crust. Spread meat mixture over the top; sprinkle with remaining cheese. Bake 5-10 minutes longer or until cheese is melted. **Yield:** 6-8 servings.

Asparagus Shepherd's Pie

(Pictured below right)

Steve Rowland, Fredericksburg, Virginia

Shepherd's pie takes a tasty twist with this version. Between the fluffy mashed potato topping and the savory ground beef base is a bed of tender, green asparagus. Even my kids ask for big helpings.

- 6 medium potatoes, peeled and quartered
- 1 pound ground beef
- 1 large onion, chopped
- 2 garlic cloves, minced
- 1 can (10-3/4 ounces) condensed cream of asparagus soup, undiluted
- 1/4 teaspoon pepper
- 1 pound fresh asparagus, trimmed and cut into 1-inch pieces
- 1/2 cup milk
- 1/4 cup butter
- 1 teaspoon rubbed sage
- 3/4 teaspoon salt
- 1/2 cup shredded mozzarella cheese
- Paprika

In a saucepan, cover potatoes with water; cook until very tender. Meanwhile, in a skillet, cook beef over medium heat until no longer pink; drain. Add the onion and garlic; cook until onion is tender. Stir in the soup and pepper; pour into a greased 2-qt. baking dish.

Cook asparagus in a small amount of water until crisp-tender, about 3-4 minutes; drain and place over beef mixture. Drain potatoes; mash with milk, butter, sage and salt. Spread over the asparagus. Sprinkle with cheese and paprika. Bake, uncovered, at 350° for 20 minutes. **Yield:** 6-8 servings.

Flip-Over Pizza

Karen Duncan, Franklin, Nebraska

Your family is sure to enjoy this easy pizza that you flip over before serving. We like it in summer when we don't want to heat up the house.

- 1 pound ground beef
- 1 celery rib, chopped
- 1 medium onion, chopped
- 1/4 cup chopped green pepper
- 1 can (10-1/2 ounces) pizza sauce
- Salt to taste
- 3/4 cup biscuit/baking mix
- 3 to 4 tablespoons milk
- 3/4 cup shredded mozzarella cheese
- 2 tablespoons grated Parmesan cheese

Crumble beef into a microwave-safe 9-in. pie plate. Sprinkle with celery, onion and green pepper. Cover and microwave on high for 7 minutes or until meat is no longer pink and vegetables are tender, stirring once; drain. Stir in the pizza sauce and salt.

Combine biscuit mix and milk just until combined. Roll out on a lightly floured surface into a 9-in. circle; place over meat mixture. Cook, uncovered, on high for 8 minutes or until a toothpick inserted into crust comes out clean. Invert onto a serving plate. Sprinkle with cheeses. **Yield:** 4 servings.

Stuffed-Crust Pizza

(Pictured below)

Renae Jacobson, Elm Creek, Nebraska

There's no pizza delivery in our rural community, so I rely on this recipe instead. The edges of the no-fail homemade crust are filled with string cheese.

     1 **pound ground beef**
     1 **small onion, chopped**
2-1/2 **to 3 cups all-purpose flour**
     2 **tablespoons Italian seasoning,** *divided*
     1 **package (1/4 ounce) quick-rise yeast**
     1 **teaspoon sugar**
   1/2 **teaspoon salt**
     1 **cup water**
     3 **tablespoons olive oil**
     3 **tablespoons cornmeal**
     4 **ounces string cheese**
     1 **can (15 ounces) pizza sauce**
   1/2 **cup sliced fresh mushrooms**
     1 **cup (4 ounces) shredded mozzarella cheese**
   1/4 **cup shredded cheddar cheese**

In a skillet, cook beef and onion until meat is no longer pink; drain and set aside. In a mixing bowl, combine 2-1/2 cups flour, 1 tablespoon Italian seasoning, yeast, sugar and salt.

In a saucepan, heat water and oil to 120°-130°. Add to the dry ingredients; beat just until moistened. Stir in enough remaining flour to form a soft dough. Let rest for 5 minutes. Sprinkle cornmeal over a greased 14-in. pizza pan.

On a lightly floured surface, roll dough into a 15-in. circle. Transfer to prepared pan, letting dough drape 1 in. over the edge. Cut string cheese in half lengthwise; place around edge of pan. Fold dough over string cheese; pinch to seal. Prick dough thoroughly with a fork. Bake at 375° for 5 minutes.

Combine pizza sauce and 2 teaspoons Italian seasoning; spread half over crust. Sprinkle with beef mixture and mushrooms; cover with remaining pizza sauce mixture. Sprinkle with shredded cheeses and remaining Italian seasoning. Bake for 18-20 minutes or until cheese is melted and crust is golden brown. **Yield:** 8 slices.

Zucchini Pizza

Lila McNamara, Dickinson, North Dakota

When zucchini is plentiful in late summer, I keep this recipe at the front of my card file. It's a wonderful way to take advantage of the season's bounty.

     4 **cups shredded peeled zucchini, drained and squeezed dry**
     2 **cups cooked rice**
1-1/2 **cups (6 ounces) shredded mozzarella cheese**
     1 **cup grated Parmesan cheese**
     2 **eggs**
     1 **pound ground beef**
     1 **medium onion, chopped**
1-1/2 **cups prepared spaghetti sauce**
     1 **teaspoon dried oregano**
   1/2 **teaspoon salt**
     2 **cups (8 ounces) shredded cheddar cheese**

In a mixing bowl, combine zucchini, rice, mozzarella cheese, Parmesan cheese and eggs until well blended. Press mixture into a greased 15-in. x 11-in. x 1-in. baking pan. Bake at 400° for 20-25 minutes or until the crust is set and lightly browned.

Meanwhile, cook ground beef and onion until meat is no longer pink; drain. Stir in spaghetti sauce, oregano and salt. Mix well. Spoon beef mixture over zucchini crust. Sprinkle with cheddar cheese. Bake at 400° for 15 minutes. Let stand 5 minutes before serving. **Yield:** 12-15 servings.

Corn Bread Hamburger Pie

(Pictured at right)

Carol Ellis, Quartzsite, Arizona

This one-dish skillet supper is a big hit. I've added green beans and other vegetables to it, and it always turns out.

- 1 pound ground beef
- 1 medium onion, chopped
- 1 medium green pepper, chopped
- 1 can (10-3/4 ounces) condensed tomato soup, undiluted
- 1/4 cup salsa
- 2 tablespoons ketchup
- 1 tablespoon steak sauce, optional
- 1 package (8-1/2 ounces) corn bread/ muffin mix

Minced fresh parsley, optional

In a 10-in. ovenproof skillet, cook the beef, onion and green pepper over medium heat until meat is no longer pink; drain. Stir in the soup, salsa, ketchup and steak sauce if desired. Prepare corn bread batter according to package directions; let stand for 2 minutes. Spoon over beef mixture. Bake at 400° for 15 minutes or until lightly browned. Sprinkle with parsley if desired. **Yield:** 4-6 servings.

til meat is no longer pink; drain. Add the eggplant, tomato sauce, parsley, oregano, salt and pepper; bring to a boil. Remove from the heat.

Prick shell with a fork. Add beef mixture. Bake at 375° for 20-25 minutes. Sprinkle with cheese. Bake 5-10 minutes until cheese is melted. Let stand 10 minutes before cutting. **Yield:** 4-6 servings.

Beef 'n' Eggplant Pie

Audrey Nemeth, Chesterville, Maine

Everyone likes eggplant when they taste it in this savory meat pie!

- 2 cups cubed eggplant
- 1/4 cup butter
- 3/4 pound ground beef
- 1/2 cup finely chopped onion
- 1 celery rib with leaves, chopped
- 1 garlic clove, minced
- 1 can (8 ounces) tomato sauce
- 1 tablespoon minced fresh parsley
- 1 tablespoon dried oregano
- 1 teaspoon salt
- 1/8 teaspoon pepper
- 1 unbaked pastry shell (9 inches)
- 1/2 to 1 cup shredded mozzarella cheese

In a small skillet, saute eggplant in butter until tender, about 5 minutes. In a large skillet, cook the beef, onion, celery and garlic over medium heat un-

Beef Pastry Pockets

Andrea Chaput, Blaine, Washington

My husband and I raise beef cattle on our farm so I'm always on the lookout for tasty recipes like this one.

- 3/4 pound ground beef
- 1-1/2 cups (6 ounces) shredded cheddar cheese
- 3/4 cup cottage cheese
- 2 eggs, lightly beaten
- 1/2 teaspoon pepper
- 1 box (17-1/4 ounces) frozen puff pastry, thawed

In a large skillet, brown beef; drain well and allow to cool. Add cheddar cheese, cottage cheese, eggs and pepper; mix well. Cut pastry into eight 5-in. squares, 1/4-in. thick. Place heaping 1/3 cupfuls of meat/cheese mixture in center of squares, folding over one edge to form a triangle. Moisten edges with water; press together with a fork to seal. Place on an ungreased baking sheet; bake at 400° for 20 minutes or until golden brown. **Yield:** 8 servings.

Meat Loaves & Meatballs

Chapter 4

Bacon-Topped Meat Loaf

(Pictured below)

Sue Call, Beech Grove, Indiana

My family loves meat loaf—this one in particular. I created the recipe after trying and adjusting many other recipes over the years. Cheddar cheese tucked inside and a flavorful bacon topping dress it up just right for Sunday dinner!

  1/2 cup chili sauce
    2 eggs, lightly beaten
    1 tablespoon Worcestershire sauce
    1 medium onion, chopped
    1 cup (4 ounces) shredded cheddar cheese
  2/3 cup dry bread crumbs
  1/2 teaspoon salt
  1/4 teaspoon pepper
    2 pounds ground beef
    2 bacon strips, halved

In a bowl, combine the first eight ingredients. Crumble beef over mixture and mix well. Shape into a loaf in an ungreased 13-in. x 9-in. x 2-in. baking dish. Top with bacon.

Bake, uncovered, at 350° for 70-80 minutes or until meat is no longer pink and a meat thermometer reads 160°. Drain; let stand for 10 minutes before cutting. **Yield:** 8 servings.

Creamy Herbed Meatballs

Marilyn Coupland, Portage la Prairie, Manitoba

Cooking isn't one of my strong points. But this recipe is one my husband frequently requests. Basil and parsley give a distinct, fresh taste.

    1 egg
  1/4 cup dry bread crumbs
  1/4 cup finely chopped onion
    1 tablespoon dried basil
  1/2 teaspoon salt
  1/2 teaspoon pepper
    1 pound ground beef
    1 can (10-3/4 ounces) condensed cream
      of mushroom soup, undiluted
  1/2 cup water
    2 tablespoons minced fresh parsley

In a large bowl, combine the first six ingredients. Crumble beef over mixture and mix well. Shape into 1-1/2-in. balls. In a large skillet, brown meatballs; drain. Stir in the remaining ingredients. Cover and simmer for 20 minutes or until the meat is no longer pink, stirring occasionally. **Yield:** 16 meatballs.

Cranberry Meat Loaf

Denise Hoover, Colorado Springs, Colorado

A tangy cranberry sauce—with the interesting ingredient of sauerkraut—gives this meat loaf a holiday zest. I have been making this recipe for years.

    3 eggs
  1/2 cup beef broth
1-1/2 cups soft bread cubes
    1 envelope onion soup mix
    3 pounds ground beef
SAUCE:
    1 can (16 ounces) whole-berry cranberry
      sauce
    1 can (14 ounces) sauerkraut, rinsed,
      drained and chopped
    1 bottle (12 ounces) chili sauce
1-1/3 cups water
  1/2 cup packed brown sugar

In a bowl, combine the first four ingredients. Crumble beef over mixture and mix well. Shape into a loaf in a greased 13-in. x 9-in. x 2-in. baking dish. In a saucepan, combine sauce ingredients. Bring to a boil; reduce heat. Simmer, uncovered, for 5 minutes.

Pour over meat loaf. Bake, uncovered, at 350° for 1-1/4 hours or until the meat is no longer pink and a meat thermometer reads 160°. **Yield:** 12 servings.

Stuffed Meat Loaf

(Pictured at right)

Shirley Leister, West Chester, Pennsylvania

I first tried this savory meat loaf recipe more than 30 years ago after seeing it demonstrated on a local TV cooking program. The savory stuffing sets it apart from the ordinary.

```
    2  eggs
    2  tablespoons milk
  1/4  cup ketchup
1-1/2  teaspoons salt
  1/8  teaspoon pepper
1-1/2  pounds ground beef
STUFFING:
  1/2  pound fresh mushrooms, sliced
    1  medium onion, chopped
    2  tablespoons butter
    2  cups soft bread crumbs
    2  tablespoons chopped fresh parsley
  1/2  teaspoon dried thyme
  1/2  teaspoon salt
  1/8  teaspoon pepper
```

In a large bowl, beat eggs, milk, ketchup, salt and pepper. Crumble beef over mixture and mix well. Pat half of the meat mixture into a greased 9-in. x 5-in. x 3-in. loaf pan; set aside.

For stuffing, saute the mushrooms and onion in butter until tender, about 3 minutes. Add bread crumbs, parsley, thyme, salt and pepper; saute until crumbs are lightly browned. Spoon over meat layer; cover with remaining meat mixture and press down gently. Bake at 350° for 1 hour or until meat is no longer pink and a meat thermometer reads 160°, draining fat when necessary. **Yield:** 6 servings.

Nacho Meatballs

June Clark, Clarkrange, Tennessee

One day, I didn't have time to cook spaghetti sauce for my meatballs. So I used canned soup as a substitute. This

dish has great cheesy flavor and a little crunch from the french-fried onions.

```
    2  eggs
  1/2  cup ketchup
    1  large onion, chopped
  2/3  cup crushed saltines (about 20 crackers)
  1/2  cup mashed potato flakes
  1/2  teaspoon garlic powder
  1/4  teaspoon pepper
    2  pounds ground beef
    1  can (11 ounces) condensed nacho
       cheese soup, undiluted
    1  can (10-3/4 ounces) condensed cream
       of mushroom soup, undiluted
1-1/3  cups water
    1  can (2.8 ounces) french-fried onions
```

In a large bowl, combine the first seven ingredients. Crumble beef over mixture and mix well. Shape into 1-1/2-in. balls. Place in a greased 13-in. x 9-in. x 2-in. baking dish. Bake, uncovered, at 350° for 1 hour, turning once; drain.

Combine soups and water; pour over meatballs. Sprinkle with onions. Bake 30 minutes longer or until meat is no longer pink. **Yield:** 30 meatballs.

meatballs. Cover and bake at 350° for 45 minutes or until meat is no longer pink. **Yield:** 8 servings.

Easy Meat Loaf

Pat Jensen, Oak Harbor, Ohio

My mother-in-law invented this recipe by mistake, but it was so well received, it became the most popular way for her to make meat loaf. With just five ingredients, it couldn't be any easier.

> 1 egg, lightly beaten
> 1 can (10-1/2 ounces) condensed French onion soup, undiluted
> 1-1/3 cups crushed butter-flavored crackers (about 33 crackers)
> 1 pound ground beef
> 1 can (10-3/4 ounces) condensed golden mushroom soup, undiluted

In a bowl, combine the egg, onion soup and cracker crumbs. Crumble beef over mixture and mix well. Shape into a loaf. Place in a greased 11-in. x 7-in. x 2-in. baking dish. Bake, uncovered, at 350° for 30 minutes.

Pour mushroom soup over loaf. Bake 1 hour longer or until meat is no longer pink and a meat thermometer reads 160°; drain. Let stand for 10 minutes before slicing. **Yield:** 4 servings.

Garden's Plenty Meatballs

(Pictured above)

Lynn Hook, Picton, Ontario

This is a wonderful dish to take to a potluck dinner. You're certain to come home with an empty dish. My sister shared the recipe with me several years ago.

> 1 egg
> 1 cup unsweetened applesauce
> 1 cup soft bread crumbs
> 2 teaspoons salt
> 1/4 teaspoon ground allspice
> 1/4 teaspoon pepper
> 2 pounds ground beef
> 1/2 cup all-purpose flour
> 3 tablespoons vegetable oil
> 1 can (28 ounces) diced tomatoes, undrained
> 1 cup sliced carrots
> 1 small green pepper, chopped
> 1 small onion, sliced

In a large bowl, combine the first six ingredients. Crumble beef over mixture and mix well. Shape into 1-1/2-in. balls. Roll in flour. In a large skillet, brown meatballs in oil; drain.

Transfer to a greased 3-qt. baking dish. Combine tomatoes, carrots, pepper and onion. Pour over

Slow-Cooked Meat Loaf

Julie Sterchi, Harrisburg, Illinois

An old standby gets fun Mexican flair and an easy new preparation method in this recipe. The round loaf gets extra flavor when served with a zippy taco sauce or chunky salsa.

> 1 egg, beaten
> 1/3 cup taco sauce
> 1 cup coarsely crushed corn chips
> 1/3 cup shredded Mexican-blend cheese
> 2 tablespoons taco seasoning
> 1/2 teaspoon salt, optional
> 2 pounds ground beef
> **Additional taco sauce *or* salsa**

In a large bowl, combine the first six ingredients. Crumble beef over mixture and mix well. Shape

When shaping meat loaves and meatballs, handle the mixture as little as possible to keep the final product light in texture. Combine all meat loaf or meatball ingredients except the ground beef. Then crumble the beef over the mixture and mix well.

The mixture for some meatballs can be very moist. If you're having a hard time shaping them, try wetting your hands.

To get a jump-start on dinner's meat loaf, combine all of the ingredients except for the beef in the morning; refrigerate. Mix in the ground beef and then bake as directed.

into a round loaf; place in a slow cooker. Cover and cook on low for 6-8 hours or until a meat thermometer reads 160°. Serve with taco sauce or salsa. **Yield:** 8 servings.

Autumn Meatballs

Helen Wiebe, Altona, Manitoba

I clipped this recipe out of the paper quite a few years ago, and it instantly became a family favorite. Tender pieces of tasty apple appear in every bite.

  2 eggs
  1 cup dry bread crumbs
  1 cup grated peeled tart apple
1/4 cup shredded cheddar cheese
  1 garlic clove, minced
  1 teaspoon salt
1/4 teaspoon pepper
1/4 teaspoon ground nutmeg
  1 pound ground beef
1-3/4 cups tomato juice
3/4 cup ketchup
1/2 cup chopped celery
1/2 teaspoon Worcestershire sauce

In a bowl, combine the first eight ingredients. Crumble beef over mixture and mix well. Shape into 1-1/2-in. balls. Place in a greased 2-qt. baking dish.

Combine the tomato juice, ketchup, celery and Worcestershire sauce; pour over meatballs. Cover and bake at 350° for 1 hour or until meat is no longer pink. **Yield:** 20 meatballs.

Pizza Meatballs

(Pictured below)

Kim Kanatzar, Blue Springs, Missouri

With mozzarella cheese inside, these tender meatballs taste almost like pizza. Whether I make them for a church potluck or a family gathering, they're a hit with all ages.

  2 cups seasoned bread crumbs
  1 cup milk
1/4 cup dried minced onion
  2 teaspoons garlic salt
1/4 teaspoon pepper
  2 pounds ground beef
  1 block (8 ounces) mozzarella cheese
1/3 cup all-purpose flour
1/4 cup vegetable oil
  2 jars (28 ounces *each*) pizza sauce

In a bowl, combine the first five ingredients; crumble beef over mixture and mix well. Shape into 48 small meatballs. Cut mozzarella into 48 cubes, 1/2 in. each; push a cube into the center of each meatball, covering the cheese completely with meat. Roll lightly in flour.

In a large skillet, cook meatballs in oil until browned; drain. Add pizza sauce; bring to a boil. Reduce heat; cover and simmer for 25-30 minutes or until the meatballs are no longer pink. **Yield:** 4 dozen.

Swedish Meatballs

(Pictured below)

Sheryl Ludeman, Kenosha, Wisconsin

This recipe relies on ingredients we always have on hand. While the meatballs cook in the microwave, boil the noodles on the stove to get this entree on the table in minutes.

- 1 small onion, chopped
- 1 egg
- 1/4 cup seasoned bread crumbs
- 2 tablespoons milk
- 1/2 teaspoon salt
- 1/8 teaspoon pepper
- 1 pound ground beef

SAUCE:
- 1 can (10-3/4 ounces) condensed cream of mushroom soup, undiluted
- 1/2 cup sour cream
- 1/4 cup milk
- 1 tablespoon dried parsley flakes
- 1/4 teaspoon ground nutmeg, optional

Hot cooked noodles

In a bowl, combine the onion, egg, bread crumbs, milk, salt and pepper. Crumble beef over mixture and mix well. Shape into 1-in. meatballs, about 24. Place in a shallow 1-1/2-qt. microwave-safe dish. Cover and microwave on high for 10 minutes or until meat is no longer pink; drain.

Combine the soup, sour cream, milk, parsley and nutmeg if desired; pour over meatballs. Cover and cook on high for 7-8 minutes or until heated through. Serve over noodles. **Yield:** 4 servings.

Barbecued Meatballs

Yvonna Nave, Lyons, Kansas

This recipe came from my home economics teacher in high school. I enjoy making it because you can cook it in the oven and still have time to do other things.

- 1 egg, lightly beaten
- 1 can (5 ounces) evaporated milk
- 1 cup quick-cooking oats
- 1/2 cup finely chopped onion
- 1 teaspoon salt
- 1 teaspoon chili powder
- 1/4 teaspoon garlic powder
- 1/4 teaspoon pepper
- 1-1/2 pounds ground beef

SAUCE:
- 1 cup ketchup
- 3/4 cup packed brown sugar
- 1/4 cup chopped onion
- 1/2 teaspoon Liquid Smoke, optional
- 1/4 teaspoon garlic powder

In a bowl, combine the first eight ingredients. Crumble beef over mixture and mix well. Shape into 1-in. balls; place in a greased 13-in. x 9-in. x 2-in. baking dish. Bake, uncovered, at 350° for 18-20 minutes or until meat is no longer pink.

Meanwhile, combine the sauce ingredients in a saucepan. Bring to a boil. Reduce heat and simmer for 2 minutes, stirring frequently. Pour over meatballs. Bake 10-12 minutes longer. **Yield:** about 4 dozen.

Microwave Onion Meat Loaves

Nicole Russman, Lincoln, Nebraska

Once I learned how to use my microwave, I found I can cook whole meals in it. This is a simple way to make individual meat loaves.

- 1 egg, beaten
- 1/3 cup milk

            2 tablespoons plus 1/4 cup barbecue
               sauce, *divided*
        1/2 cup crushed stuffing
            1 tablespoon onion soup mix
      1-1/4 pounds ground beef

In a bowl, combine egg, milk, 2 tablespoons barbecue sauce, stuffing and soup mix. Crumble beef
over mixture; mix well. Shape into five loaves;
arrange around edge of a microwave-safe dish.

   Microwave, uncovered, on high for 6-7 minutes
or until a meat thermometer reads 160°. Cover and
let stand for 5-10 minutes. Top with the remaining
barbecue sauce. **Yield:** 5 servings.

Spinach Meat Roll

Gail Buss, Westminster, Maryland

*My family loves spinach. We're lucky to have a friend
who grows plenty and shares with us. Our favorite way
to serve it is in this meat roll.*

            2 eggs
        3/4 cup seasoned bread crumbs
        1/3 cup ketchup
        1/4 cup milk
            1 teaspoon salt, *divided*
        1/4 teaspoon pepper
        1/4 teaspoon dried oregano
            2 pounds ground beef
            1 package (10 ounces) frozen leaf
               spinach, thawed and drained
        1/2 pound thinly sliced fully cooked ham
            2 cups (8 ounces) shredded mozzarella
               cheese, *divided*

In a bowl, lightly beat the eggs; add bread crumbs,
ketchup, milk, 1/2 teaspoon salt, pepper and
oregano. Crumble beef over mixture and mix well.
On a large piece of heavy-duty foil, pat beef mixture into a 12-in. x 10-in. rectangle. Cover with
spinach to within 1/2 in. of edges. Sprinkle with remaining salt. Top with ham and 1-1/2 cups cheese.

   Roll up jelly-roll style, starting with a short side
and peeling foil away while rolling. Seal seam and
ends; place with seam side down in a greased 15-
in. x 10-in. x 1-in. baking pan. Bake, uncovered, at
350° for 1 hour and 10 minutes or until meat is no
longer pink and a meat thermometer reads 160°.
Top with remaining cheese; bake 5 minutes longer
or until cheese is melted. **Yield:** 8 servings.

Li'l Cheddar Meat Loaves

(Pictured above)

Katy Bowron, Cocolalla, Idaho

*I got this recipe from my aunt when I was a teen and
have made these lip-smacking miniature loaves many
times. My husband and three children count this main
dish among their favorites.*

            1 egg
        3/4 cup milk
            1 cup (4 ounces) shredded cheddar cheese
        1/2 cup quick-cooking oats
        1/2 cup chopped onion
            1 teaspoon salt
            1 pound ground beef
        2/3 cup ketchup
        1/2 cup packed brown sugar
      1-1/2 teaspoons prepared mustard

In a bowl, beat the egg and milk. Stir in cheese,
oats, onion and salt. Crumble beef over mixture and
mix well. Shape into eight loaves; place in a greased
13-in. x 9-in. x 2-in. baking dish. Combine ketchup,
brown sugar and mustard; spoon over loaves.

   Bake, uncovered, at 350° for 45 minutes or until
the meat is no longer pink and a meat thermometer reads 160°. **Yield:** 8 servings.

maining spaghetti sauce; bake 10 minutes longer. Let stand for 10 minutes before slicing. **Yield:** 6 servings.

Editor's Note: 3 ounces of mozzarella cheese, cut into 4-in. x 1/2-in. sticks, may be substituted.

Reunion Meatballs

Toni King, London, Kentucky

Whenever we attend a picnic or family get-together, people expect me to bring these saucy meatballs and copies of the recipe.

> 1/2 cup milk
>   1 egg
>   1 medium onion, chopped
>   3 bacon strips, cooked and crumbled
> 1/2 cup crushed saltines (about 15 crackers)
>   2 teaspoons salt
> 1-1/2 pounds ground beef
> 1/2 pound bulk pork sausage
> SAUCE:
>   1 bottle (14 ounces) ketchup
> 1-1/4 cups water
> 1/2 cup vinegar
> 1/2 cup packed brown sugar
>   1 medium onion, chopped
>   1 tablespoon chili powder
> 1-1/2 teaspoons Worcestershire sauce
> Dash salt

In a large bowl, combine the first six ingredients. Crumble beef and sausage over mixture and mix well. Shape into 1-1/2-in. balls. Place in a greased 13-in. x 9-in. x 2-in. baking dish.

In a saucepan, combine the sauce ingredients. Bring to a boil; reduce heat. Simmer, uncovered, for

---

String Cheese Meat Loaf

(Pictured above and on page 52)

Laura Lawrence, Salinas, California

My daughter likes the cheese stuffed into this meat loaf made with a blend of ground beef and Italian sausage. Served with a salad and sourdough bread, the meal is special enough for company.

>   1 cup meatless spaghetti sauce, *divided*
>   1 egg, lightly beaten
>   1 cup seasoned bread crumbs
>   2 garlic cloves, minced
> 1-1/2 teaspoons dried rosemary, crushed
>   1 pound ground beef
>   8 ounces bulk Italian sausage
>   3 pieces string cheese

In a bowl, combine 1/2 cup spaghetti sauce, egg, bread crumbs, garlic and rosemary. Crumble meat over mixture and mix well. Press half into a greased 8-in. x 4-in. x 2-in. loaf pan. Place two pieces of cheese, side by side, near one end of loaf. Cut the remaining piece of cheese in half; place side by side on opposite end of loaf. Top with remaining meat mixture; press down firmly to seal.

Bake, uncovered, at 350° for 1-1/4 to 1-1/2 hours or until meat is no longer pink and a meat thermometer reads 160°; drain. Drizzle with the re-

---

Making Meatballs

To make meatballs of equal size, lightly pat the mixture into a 1-inch-thick rectangle. Using a knife, cut the rectangle into the number of meatballs needed for the recipe. Gently roll each square into a ball.

Or, if you have a 1-1/2- or 1-3/4-inch-diameter scoop, scoop the mixture into equal sized portions. Gently roll each into a ball.

5 minutes. Pour over meatballs. Bake, uncovered, at 350° for 1-1/2 hours or until meat is no longer pink. **Yield:** 40 meatballs.

Tangy Meatballs Over Noodles

Teri Lindquist, Gurnee, Illinois

These moist meatballs are so easy to make, yet they taste so fancy. The sweet and tangy sauce has surprising flavor from ginger and cloves.

   1 **egg, lightly beaten**
 1/3 **cup milk**
 1/4 **cup seasoned bread crumbs**
   1 **tablespoon dried minced onion**
   1 **teaspoon salt**
1-1/2 **pounds ground beef**
   2 **cans (14-3/4 ounces *each*) beef gravy**
 1/2 **cup packed brown sugar**
 1/4 **cup cider vinegar**
 3/4 **teaspoon ground ginger**
 1/4 **teaspoon ground cloves**
   1 **package (12 ounces) egg noodles**

In a bowl, combine the first five ingredients. Crumble beef over mixture and mix well. Shape into 1-1/2-in. balls. Place 1 in. apart in greased 15-in. x 10-in. x 1-in. baking pans. Bake, uncovered, at 350° for 20 minutes.

With a slotted spoon, transfer meatballs to a greased 2-1/2-qt. baking dish. Combine gravy, brown sugar, vinegar, ginger and cloves; pour over meatballs. Cover and bake 30 minutes longer or until meat is no longer pink. Meanwhile, cook noodles according to package directions; drain. Serve with meatballs. **Yield:** 8 servings (40 meatballs).

Sweet-and-Sour Meat Loaf

(Pictured at right)

Deb Thompson, Lincoln, Nebraska

I combined a few great-tasting meat loaf recipes to create this wonderful family favorite. My husband loves it, and because it's made in the microwave, it's ideal for busy nights.

   1 **egg**
   5 **tablespoons ketchup, *divided***
   2 **tablespoons prepared mustard**
 1/2 **cup dry bread crumbs**
   2 **tablespoons onion soup mix**
 1/4 **teaspoon salt**
 1/4 **teaspoon pepper**
   1 **pound ground beef**
 1/4 **cup sugar**
   2 **tablespoons brown sugar**
   2 **tablespoons cider vinegar**

In a bowl, lightly beat the egg. Add 2 tablespoons of ketchup, mustard, bread crumbs, soup mix, salt and pepper. Crumble beef over mixture and mix well. Shape into an oval loaf.

Place in a shallow 1-qt. microwave-safe dish; cover with waxed paper. Microwave on high for 11-12 minutes or until meat is no longer pink, rotating a half turn once; drain.

In a small bowl, combine the sugars, vinegar and remaining ketchup; drizzle over the meat loaf. Cover and microwave on high for 3-5 minutes or until meat is no longer pink. Let meat loaf stand for 10 minutes before slicing. **Yield:** 4 servings.

Meat Loaf Miniatures

(Pictured below)

Joyce Wegmann, Burlington, Iowa

I do not usually like meat loaf, but my family and I can't get enough of these little muffins topped with a sweet ketchup sauce. They are the perfect portion size. This recipe requires no chopping, so it's quick and easy to make a double batch and have extras for another day.

      1 **cup ketchup**
      3 **to 4 tablespoons packed brown sugar**
      1 **teaspoon ground mustard**
      2 **eggs, beaten**
      4 **teaspoons Worcestershire sauce**
      3 **cups Crispix cereal, crushed**
      3 **teaspoons onion powder**
  1/2 **to 1 teaspoon seasoned salt**
  1/2 **teaspoon garlic powder**
  1/2 **teaspoon pepper**
      3 **pounds ground beef**

In a large bowl, combine ketchup, brown sugar and mustard. Remove 1/2 cup for topping; set aside. Add eggs, Worcestershire sauce, cereal and seasonings to remaining ketchup mixture; mix well. Let stand for 5 minutes. Crumble beef over cereal

mixture and mix well.

Press meat mixture into 18 greased muffin cups (about 1/3 cup each). Bake at 375° for 18-20 minutes. Drizzle with reserved ketchup mixture; bake 10 minutes longer or until meat is no longer pink and a meat thermometer reads 160°.

Serve desired number of meat loaves. Cool remaining loaves; freeze. Transfer to freezer bags; freeze for up to 3 months. **Yield:** 1-1/2 dozen.

To use frozen meat loaves: Completely thaw in the refrigerator. Place loaves in a greased baking dish. Bake at 350° for 30 minutes or until heated through, or cover and microwave on high for 1 minute or until heated through.

Italian Meat Loaf

Lisa Malone, Cordell, Oklahoma

I received the recipe for this moist meat loaf in my high school home economics class. At the time, I made it for my mom and dad. Now I fix it for my husband and daughter.

      1 **egg, beaten**
      1 **can (8 ounces) tomato sauce, *divided***
  1/2 **cup dry bread crumbs**
  1/2 **cup finely chopped onion, optional**
  1/2 **cup finely chopped green pepper, optional**
      1 **teaspoon dried oregano, *divided***
      1 **teaspoon salt**
  1/8 **teaspoon pepper**
  1-1/2 **pounds ground beef**
  1/2 **cup shredded mozzarella cheese**
      2 **tablespoons grated Parmesan cheese**

In a bowl, combine the egg, half of the tomato sauce, bread crumbs, onion and green pepper if desired, 1/2 teaspoon of oregano, salt and pepper. Crumble beef over mixture and mix well.

On a large piece of heavy-duty foil, pat meat mixture into a 14-in. x 8-in. rectangle. Sprinkle cheeses to within 1/2 in. of edges. Roll up, jelly-roll style, starting with a short side and peeling foil away while rolling. Seal seam and ends.

Transfer to a microwave-safe 9-in. x 5-in. x 3-in. loaf pan. Microwave, uncovered, at 50% power for 12 minutes, rotating a half turn once; drain. Continue cooking on 50% power for 20 minutes or until meat is no longer pink, rotating a half turn once.

In a bowl, combine the remaining tomato sauce and oregano. Pour over meat loaf. Microwave, uncovered, on high for 2 minutes. Cover loosely with foil; let stand 5 minutes before serving. **Yield:** 6 servings.

Reuben Meat Loaf

Mary Alice Taylor, Downingtown, Pennsylvania

This moist loaf is sure to become a favorite with sauerkraut lovers. I roll tangy kraut, Swiss cheese and Thousand Island salad dressing into well-seasoned ground beef for a delicious dinner.

  1　egg, lightly beaten
  1　medium onion, chopped
  1/4　cup sweet pickle relish
  1　tablespoon Worcestershire sauce
  1　cup soft rye bread crumbs
  1/2　teaspoon salt
  1/4　teaspoon pepper
  2　pounds ground beef
  1/4　cup Thousand Island salad dressing
  1　can (8 ounces) sauerkraut, rinsed and drained
  1　cup (4 ounces) shredded Swiss cheese, *divided*

In a large bowl, combine the first seven ingredients. Crumble beef over mixture and mix well. On a piece of heavy-duty aluminum foil, pat meat mixture into a 14-in. x 10-in. rectangle. Spread with salad dressing; top with sauerkraut and 1/2 cup Swiss cheese. Roll up, starting with a long side and peeling foil away while rolling; seal seams and ends.

Place in a greased 15-in. x 10-in. x 1-in. baking pan. Bake, uncovered, at 350° for 50-55 minutes or until meat is no longer pink and a meat thermometer reads 160°; drain. Sprinkle with remaining cheese. Bake 2 minutes longer or until cheese is melted. Let stand 10 minutes before slicing. **Yield:** 8 servings.

Food Safety

Thoroughly wash all equipment and your hands before and after handling uncooked ground beef.

Veggie Meatball Medley

(Pictured above)

Barbara Kernohan, Forest, Ontario

I developed this recipe in an attempt to offer a simple, well-balanced meal the whole family could enjoy. Everyone raves about the tasty sauce.

  1　egg
  1/4　cup dry bread crumbs
  1/2　teaspoon salt
  1/4　teaspoon pepper
  1　pound ground beef
  2　cups frozen stir-fry vegetable blend
  1　medium onion, chopped
  1　can (10-3/4 ounces) condensed cream of mushroom soup, undiluted
  1/4　cup soy sauce
  1/4　teaspoon garlic powder
Hot cooked rice

In a large bowl, combine the first four ingredients. Crumble beef over mixture and mix well. Shape into 1-1/2-in. balls.

In a large nonstick skillet, cook meatballs, vegetables and onion until meatballs are browned; drain. Stir in the soup, soy sauce and garlic powder. Bring to a boil. Reduce heat; simmer, uncovered, for 20 minutes or until the meat is no longer pink, stirring occasionally. Serve over rice. **Yield:** 4 servings.

cheese aside. Roll up loaf, jelly-roll style, starting with a short side and pulling away waxed paper while rolling. Seal seams and ends well. Place loaf, seam side down, in a greased 11-in. x 7-in. x 2-in. baking pan.

Bake at 350° for 45 minutes or until meat is no longer pink and a meat thermometer reads 160°. Cut the reserved cheese slices in half diagonally; place on top of loaf. Return to the oven for 5 minutes or until cheese is melted. Let stand for 10 minutes before slicing. **Yield:** 6 servings.

Spaghetti and Meatballs

Dawnetta McGhee, Lewiston, Idaho

When you have time, simmer some of this hearty sauce with home-style meatballs. It makes a memorable main course you'll rely on for years to come.

    1 large onion, finely chopped
    2 garlic cloves, minced
    2 tablespoons olive oil
    3 cans (10-3/4 ounces *each*) tomato puree
    1 can (12 ounces) tomato paste
1-1/2 cups water
  1/4 cup grated Parmesan cheese
    1 tablespoon dried oregano
    1 tablespoon salt
    1 tablespoon sugar
MEATBALLS:
  3/4 cup finely crushed saltines
    4 eggs, beaten
    2 garlic cloves, minced
    3 tablespoons grated Parmesan cheese
    1 teaspoon dried oregano
    1 pound ground beef
  1/4 pound ground pork
Hot cooked spaghetti

In a Dutch oven, saute onion and garlic in oil until tender. Add the next seven ingredients; mix well. Simmer, uncovered, for 1-1/2 hours.

Meanwhile, combine cracker crumbs, eggs, garlic, Parmesan cheese and oregano in a large bowl. Crumble beef and pork over mixture; mix well. Shape into 1-1/2-in. balls; brown in a skillet, turning once.

Add to sauce; simmer, uncovered, 1-1/2 hours longer or until meat is no longer pink. Serve over spaghetti. **Yield:** 6-8 servings.

Cheeseburger Meat Loaf

(Pictured above)

Paula Sullivan, Barker, New York

I created this meat loaf one day when I wanted to make cheeseburgers—my husband's favorite—but it was too chilly to grill outside. I've served it numerous times since then, and it never fails to get rave reviews. Even your most finicky eater will enjoy this meaty main dish.

  1/2 cup ketchup, *divided*
    1 egg
  1/4 cup dry bread crumbs
    1 teaspoon onion powder
    1 pound ground beef
    2 teaspoons prepared mustard
    2 teaspoons dill pickle relish
    6 slices process American cheese

In a bowl, combine 1/4 cup ketchup, egg, bread crumbs and onion powder. Crumble beef over mixture and mix well.

On a large piece of waxed paper, pat beef mixture into a 10-in. x 6-in. rectangle. Spread remaining ketchup over meat to within 1/2 in. of long sides and 1-1/2 in. of short sides. Top with mustard and relish.

Place four cheese slices on top; set remaining

Wild Rice Meat Loaf

Genie Lang, Jamestown, North Dakota

I've shared this recipe with many friends. The unique, hearty meat loaf is full of surprises—tangy wild rice and pockets of cheddar cheese make it extra special.

    4 cups cooked wild rice
    2 cups (8 ounces) shredded cheddar
      cheese
    1 cup dry bread crumbs
    1 cup finely chopped onion
  1/2 cup all-purpose flour
    2 eggs, beaten
1-1/4 teaspoons salt
    1 teaspoon rubbed sage
  3/4 teaspoon pepper
    1 pound ground beef

Combine first nine ingredients in a large bowl; crumble beef over mixture and mix well. Firmly press into a greased 9-in. x 5-in. x 3-in. loaf pan.

Bake, uncovered, at 350° for 70 minutes or until meat is no longer pink and a meat thermometer reads 160°. Cover with foil during the last 15 minutes if the top is browning too quickly. **Yield:** 4-6 servings.

Apricot Meatballs

Lorenda Spain, Dumas, Texas

This is one of my husband's favorite recipes using ground beef. It makes an easy Sunday dinner, and the sauce gets a hint of sweetness from apricot preserves.

    1 egg
    1 cup soft bread crumbs
  1/4 cup chopped onion
    1 teaspoon salt
    1 pound ground beef
  1/2 cup apricot preserves
  1/4 cup barbecue sauce

In a bowl, combine the first four ingredients. Crumble beef over mixture and mix well. Shape into 1-in. balls. In a skillet, brown the meatballs in several batches, then drain. Transfer to a greased 2-qt. baking dish.

Combine preserves and barbecue sauce; pour over meatballs. Cover and bake at 350° for 30 minutes or until the meat is no longer pink. **Yield:** 38 meatballs.

Favorite Meat Loaf Cups

(Pictured below)

Sue Gronholz, Columbus, Wisconsin

My family enjoys meat loaf, but sometimes I can't spare the hour or more it takes to bake in the traditional shape. A quick alternative is to divide the meat mixture into muffin cups for individual servings that are ready in less than 30 minutes.

    2 eggs, beaten
  1/4 cup milk
  1/4 cup ketchup
  1/2 cup crushed cornflakes
    4 tablespoons dried minced onion
    1 teaspoon prepared mustard
    1 teaspoon salt
  1/4 teaspoon pepper
    2 pounds ground beef
Additional ketchup, optional

In a large bowl, combine the first eight ingredients. Crumble beef over mixture and mix well. Press into 12 foil-lined or greased muffin cups. Bake at 350° for 25 minutes or until the meat is no longer pink. Drain before serving. Drizzle with ketchup if desired. **Yield:** 6 servings.

Meat Loaf Wellington

(Pictured below)

Wanda Orton, Emporia, Kansas

My family would rather have this eye-appealing loaf than plain meat loaf. It's a good way to dress up an ordinary dish for company. Many people have asked for the recipe over the years.

    1 **can (10-1/2 ounces) beef gravy,** *divided*
1-1/2 **cups cubed day-old bread**
  1/4 **cup chopped onion**
    1 **egg**
    1 **teaspoon salt**
    2 **pounds ground beef**
    1 **tube (8 ounces) refrigerated crescent rolls**

In a bowl, combine 1/4 cup gravy, bread cubes, onion, egg and salt. Crumble beef over mixture and mix well. Press into a greased 9-in. x 5-in. x 3-in. loaf pan.

Bake, uncovered, at 375° for 1 hour or until the meat is no longer pink and a meat thermometer reads 160°. Remove meat loaf from pan; drain on paper towels.

Place on a greased 13-in. x 9-in. x 2-in. baking pan. Unroll the crescent roll dough and seal the perforations. Cover the top and sides of meat loaf with the dough; trim any excess.

Bake the meat loaf 10-15 minutes longer or until the pastry is golden brown. Heat the remaining gravy and serve it warm with the meat loaf. **Yield:** 6-8 servings.

Meatballs with Cream Sauce

Michelle Thompson, Smithfield, Utah

I get raves from my husband and even our three fussy children when I serve these satisfying meatballs with mashed potatoes. The savory cream sauce gives a tasty new twist to the meatballs and always makes this a memorable main dish.

    1 **egg, lightly beaten**
  1/4 **cup milk**
    2 **tablespoons ketchup**
    1 **teaspoon Worcestershire sauce**
  3/4 **cup quick-cooking oats**
  1/4 **cup finely chopped onion**
  1/4 **cup minced fresh parsley**
    1 **teaspoon salt**
  1/4 **teaspoon pepper**
1-1/2 **pounds ground beef**
    3 **tablespoons all-purpose flour**
CREAM SAUCE:
    2 **tablespoons butter**
    2 **tablespoons all-purpose flour**
  1/4 **teaspoon dried thyme**
Salt and pepper to taste
    1 **can (14 ounces) chicken broth**
  2/3 **cup heavy whipping cream**
    2 **tablespoons minced fresh parsley**

In a bowl, combine the first nine ingredients. Crumble beef over mixture and mix well. Shape into 1-1/2-in. balls. Roll in flour, shaking off excess. Place 1 in. apart on greased 15-in. x 10-in. x 1-in. baking pans.

Bake, uncovered, at 400° for 10 minutes. Turn meatballs; bake 12-15 minutes longer or until meat is no longer pink.

Meanwhile, for sauce, melt butter in a saucepan over medium heat. Stir in flour, thyme, salt and pepper until smooth. Gradually add broth and cream; bring to a boil. Cook and stir for 2 minutes or until thickened and bubbly.

Drain meatballs on paper towels; transfer to a

serving dish. Top with sauce; sprinkle with parsley. **Yield:** 6 servings.

Meat Loaf Potato Surprise

Lois Edwards, Citrus Heights, California

Although I'm retired, my days continue to be full. So easy dishes like this are a blessing to me.

   1 **cup soft bread crumbs**
 1/2 **cup beef broth**
   1 **egg, beaten**
   4 **teaspoons dried minced onion**
   1 **teaspoon salt**
 1/4 **teaspoon Italian seasoning**
 1/4 **teaspoon pepper**
1-1/2 **pounds ground beef**
   4 **cups frozen shredded hash browns, thawed**
 1/3 **cup grated Parmesan cheese**
 1/4 **cup minced fresh parsley**
   1 **teaspoon onion salt**
SAUCE:
   1 **can (8 ounces) tomato sauce**
 1/4 **cup beef broth**
   2 **teaspoons prepared mustard**
Additional Parmesan cheese, optional

In a bowl, combine crumbs, broth, egg and seasonings; let stand for 2 minutes. Crumble beef over mixture and mix well. On a piece of waxed paper, pat meat mixture into a 10 in. square.

Combine hash browns, cheese, parsley and onion salt; spoon over meat. Roll up, jelly-roll style, removing waxed paper as you roll. Pinch edges and ends to seal; place with seam side down in an ungreased shallow baking pan.

Bake at 375° for 40 minutes or until a meat is no longer pink and meat thermometer reads 160°. Combine the first three sauce ingredients; spoon over loaf. Return to the oven for 10 minutes. Sprinkle with Parmesan if desired. **Yield:** 8 servings.

Meatballs with Pepper Sauce

(Pictured above right)

Julie Neal, Green Bay, Wisconsin

I've found these colorful meatballs hold up well in a slow cooker for a no-fuss potluck dish. Folks always go back for seconds. At home, we enjoy them served over rice or noodles.

   1 **cup evaporated milk**
   1 **tablespoon Worcestershire sauce**
   1 **envelope onion soup mix**
   2 **pounds ground beef**
SAUCE:
 1/2 **pound fresh mushrooms, sliced**
1-1/2 **cups ketchup**
 3/4 **cup packed brown sugar**
 3/4 **cup water**
 1/2 **cup chopped green pepper**
 1/2 **cup chopped sweet red pepper**
   2 **tablespoons chopped onion**
   1 **tablespoon Worcestershire sauce**

In a large bowl, combine the first three ingredients. Crumble beef over mixture and mix well. Shape into 1-in. balls. Place on a greased broiler pan. Broil 4-6 in. from the heat for 5-8 minutes or until browned.

In a Dutch oven, combine all of the sauce ingredients. Bring to a boil. Reduce heat and add the meatballs. Simmer, uncovered, for 1 hour or until meat is no longer pink. **Yield:** 60 meatballs.

For sauce, combine brown sugar and cornstarch in the skillet. Stir in pineapple with juice, vinegar and soy sauce. Bring to a boil, stirring constantly. Reduce heat; cover and simmer for about 10 minutes or until sauce thickens, stirring occasionally. Add green pepper; cover and simmer until tender, about 5 minutes. Return meatballs to skillet and heat through. **Yield:** 4-6 servings.

Grilled Meat Loaf

Catherine Carpenter, Barnesville, Ohio

Grilled Meat Loaf is the perfect summertime twist on a comforting family favorite. I shape the meat mixture into loaves and "bake" them on the grill.

- 1/2 cup ketchup
- 1/2 cup quick-cooking oats
- 1/4 cup chopped green pepper
-   1 egg
-   1 teaspoon dried parsley flakes
-   1 teaspoon Worcestershire sauce
- 1/2 teaspoon garlic powder
- 1/2 teaspoon dried basil
- 1/4 teaspoon pepper
-   2 pounds ground beef
Additional ketchup, optional

In a large bowl, combine the first nine ingredients. Crumble beef over mixture and mix well. Shape into two loaves. Place a sheet of heavy-duty foil in center of grill. Place meat loaves on foil (do not seal foil).

Grill, covered, over indirect medium heat for 50 minutes or until meat is no longer pink and a meat thermometer reads 160°. Brush tops with additional ketchup if desired. Let stand for 10 minutes before slicing. **Yield:** 2 loaves (4 servings each).

Oven Porcupines

Shelly Ryun, Malvern, Iowa

I've always remembered these from my school days…so I searched until I found the recipe that was just like I remembered. This is it!

- 1/2 cup uncooked long grain rice
- 1/2 cup water
- 1/3 cup chopped onion

Sweet-and-Sour Meatballs

(Pictured above)

Cathy MacPherson, Prescott, Ontario

We raise our own beef cattle, so there's always plenty of ground beef on hand. I enjoy preparing this dish, because I know there will be no leftovers. Plus, these meatballs are as attractive as they are delicious.

-   1 egg, beaten
- 1/4 cup milk
- 1/2 cup dry bread crumbs
-   2 tablespoons finely chopped onion
- 3/4 teaspoon salt
- 1/2 teaspoon Worcestershire sauce
-   1 pound ground beef
SAUCE:
- 1/2 cup packed brown sugar
-   2 tablespoons cornstarch
-   1 can (20 ounces) pineapple chunks, undrained
- 1/3 cup vinegar
-   1 tablespoon soy sauce
-   1 medium green pepper, cut into bite-size pieces

Mix together first six ingredients; crumble beef over mixture and mix well. Shape into 1-1/2-in. balls. In a skillet, cook meatballs until no longer pink, turning often; remove and set aside. Drain.

        1 teaspoon salt
    1/4 teaspoon garlic powder
    1/2 teaspoon pepper
        1 pound ground beef
        1 can (15 ounces) tomato sauce
        1 cup water
        2 teaspoons Worcestershire sauce

Combine first six ingredients. Crumble beef over mixture and mix well. Shape into 12 balls. Place meatballs in an ungreased 8-in square baking dish. Combine remaining ingredients; pour over meatballs. Cover with foil and bake at 350° for 1 hour. Uncover; bake 15 minutes longer. **Yield:** 4 servings.

Unstuffed Cabbage

(Pictured below right)

Mrs. Bernard Snow, Lewiston, Michigan

Here is one of my favorite ways to cook and enjoy cabbage. It has all the good flavor of regular cabbage rolls, but it's a lot less bother to make.

TOMATO SAUCE:
        1 large onion, chopped
        1 medium head cabbage, coarsely chopped (about 8 cups)
        1 can (8 ounces) tomato sauce
        1 can (28 ounces) diced tomatoes, undrained
        1 cup water
    1/4 cup lemon juice
    1/3 cup raisins
MEATBALLS:
    1/2 cup uncooked long grain rice
        1 teaspoon Worcestershire sauce
    1/2 teaspoon salt
    1/4 teaspoon pepper
        1 pound ground beef

Combine all of the sauce ingredients in a large skillet or Dutch oven. Bring to a boil; reduce heat and simmer.

Meanwhile, combine first four meatball ingredients; crumble beef over mixture and mix well. Shape into 36 balls, about 1-1/4 in. in diameter. Add to simmering sauce. Cover and simmer about 45 minutes or until the cabbage is tender. Uncover and cook about 15 minutes longer or until sauce thickens. **Yield:** 6-8 servings.

Meat Loaf for a Mob

Niki Reese Eschen, Santa Maria, California

Our small synagogue has two teams that alternate with churches of various denominations and civic organizations to provide meals at a homeless shelter. This tasty satisfying meat loaf is well liked there.

        8 eggs, beaten
        1 can (46 ounces) V8 juice
        2 large onions, finely chopped
        4 celery ribs, finely chopped
    4-1/4 cups seasoned bread crumbs
        2 envelopes onion soup mix
        2 teaspoons pepper
        8 pounds ground beef
    3/4 cup ketchup
    1/3 cup packed brown sugar
    1/4 cup prepared mustard

In a very large bowl, combine the eggs, V8 juice, onions, celery, bread crumbs, soup mix and pepper. Crumble beef over mixture; mix well. Shape into four loaves; place each loaf in a greased 13-in. x 9-in. x 2-in. baking dish. Bake, uncovered, at 350° for 45 minutes.

Meanwhile, combine the ketchup, brown sugar and mustard. Spread over loaves. Bake 15 minutes longer or until a meat thermometer reads 160°. **Yield:** 4 meat loaves (8 servings each).

Casseroles

Chapter 5

400° for 15 minutes. Reduce heat to 350°; bake about 1 hour longer or until vegetables are tender and meat is no longer pink. Sprinkle with cheese; cover and let stand until melted. **Yield:** 6-8 servings.

Fiesta Macaroni

Sandra Castillo, Sun Prairie, Wisconsin

This dish is so easy to fix, and everyone loves the zesty flavor that the salsa and chili beans provide.

> 1 package (16 ounces) elbow macaroni
> 1 pound ground beef
> 1 jar (16 ounces) salsa
> 10 ounces process cheese (Velveeta), cubed
> 1 can (15 ounces) chili-style beans

Cook macaroni according to package directions. Meanwhile, in a skillet, cook beef over medium heat until no longer pink; drain. Drain macaroni; set aside.

In a microwave-safe bowl, combine salsa and cheese. Microwave, uncovered, on high for 3-4 minutes or until cheese is melted. Stir into the skillet; add the macaroni and beans. Transfer to a greased 13-in. x 9-in. x 2-in. baking dish. Bake, uncovered, at 350° for 30-35 minutes or until heated through. **Yield:** 6-8 servings.

Vegetable Beef Casserole

(Pictured above)

Evangeline Rew, Manassas, Virginia

This easy one-dish recipe has been a family favorite ever since it was handed down to me over 40 years ago from my husband's aunt. Add whatever vegetables you have on hand. A simple salad goes nicely with this dish.

> 3 medium unpeeled potatoes, sliced
> 3 carrots, sliced
> 3 celery ribs, sliced
> 2 cups fresh or frozen green beans
> 1 medium onion, chopped
> 1 pound ground beef
> 1 teaspoon dried thyme
> 1 teaspoon salt
> 1 teaspoon pepper
> 4 medium tomatoes, peeled, seeded and chopped
> 1 cup (4 ounces) shredded cheddar cheese

In a 3-qt. casserole, layer half of the potatoes, carrots, celery, green beans and onion. Crumble half of the uncooked beef over vegetables. Sprinkle with 1/2 teaspoon each of thyme, salt and pepper. Repeat layers. Top with tomatoes. Cover and bake at

Cheesy Beef Tetrazzini

Gladys Van Beek, Lynden, Washington

It won't be long before this hearty casserole becomes a mainstay. My gang loves it for the flavor. I love it because it's simple to make and can be assembled the night before serving.

> 1-1/2 pounds ground beef
> 1 small onion, chopped
> 1 can (15 ounces) tomato sauce
> 1/2 to 1 teaspoon salt
> 1/4 teaspoon pepper
> 1 package (8 ounces) cream cheese, softened
> 1 cup small-curd cottage cheese
> 1 cup (8 ounces) sour cream
> 1/4 cup chopped green pepper
> 1/4 cup thinly sliced green onions

1 package (7 ounces) thin spaghetti,
cooked and drained
1/4 cup grated Parmesan cheese

In a large skillet, cook beef and onion over medium heat until meat is no longer pink; drain. Stir in tomato sauce, salt and pepper; bring to a boil. Reduce heat; simmer, uncovered, for 5 minutes.

In a mixing bowl, beat cream cheese, cottage cheese and sour cream until blended. Stir in green pepper, onions and spaghetti. Transfer to a greased 2-1/2-qt. baking dish. Top with beef mixture. Sprinkle with Parmesan cheese. Bake, uncovered, at 350° for 30-35 minutes or until bubbly. **Yield:** 6 servings.

Hearty Hamburger Casserole

Faith Richards, Tampa, Florida

I need just a few ingredients to pack a lot of flavor into this hearty ground beef bake. My daughter received this recipe from a missionary when they were both serving in Zambia.

5 medium potatoes, peeled and sliced
1 small onion, chopped
1 pound ground beef
1 can (10-3/4 ounces) condensed cream of mushroom soup, undiluted
1 can (10-1/2 ounces) condensed vegetarian vegetable soup, undiluted
1 cup crushed potato chips

In a greased 13-in. x 9 in. x 2-in. baking dish, layer the potatoes and onion. Crumble beef over onion. Spread soups over beef.

Cover and bake at 350° for 55 minutes. Uncover; sprinkle with chips. Bake 20 minutes longer or until meat is no longer pink. **Yield:** 4-6 servings.

Spinach Beef Macaroni Bake

(Pictured at right)

Lois Lauppe, Lahoma, Oklahoma

This hearty casserole is great for a family reunion or church supper. I've also made half the recipe for family gatherings. It's become a special request of my grandson-in-law and great-grandson, so I often serve it when they're visiting.

5-1/4 cups uncooked elbow macaroni
2-1/2 pounds ground beef
2 large onions, chopped
3 large carrots, shredded
3 celery ribs, chopped
2 cans (28 ounces *each*) Italian diced tomatoes, undrained
4 teaspoons salt
1 teaspoon garlic powder
1 teaspoon pepper
1/2 teaspoon dried oregano
2 packages (10 ounces *each*) frozen chopped spinach, thawed and squeezed dry
1 cup grated Parmesan cheese

Cook macaroni according to package directions. Meanwhile, in a Dutch oven or large kettle, cook the beef, onions, carrots and celery over medium heat until meat is no longer pink; drain. Add the tomatoes, salt, garlic powder, pepper and oregano. Bring to a boil. Reduce heat; cover and simmer for 30 minutes or until vegetables are tender.

Drain macaroni; add macaroni and spinach to beef mixture. Pour into two greased 3-qt. baking dishes. Sprinkle with Parmesan cheese. Bake, uncovered, at 350° for 25-30 minutes or until heated through. **Yield:** 2 casseroles (12 servings each).

Dinner in a Dish

(Pictured below)

Betty Sitzman, Wray, Colorado

I haven't found anyone yet who can resist this saucy beef casserole topped with mashed potatoes. The peas and tomatoes add color and make a helping or two a complete meal.

       2 pounds ground beef
       1 medium onion, chopped
       2 cans (14-1/2 ounces each) diced
          tomatoes, undrained
       3 cups frozen peas
     2/3 cup ketchup
     1/4 cup chopped fresh parsley
       2 tablespoons all-purpose flour
       2 teaspoons beef bouillon granules
       2 teaspoons dried marjoram
       1 teaspoon salt
     1/2 teaspoon pepper
       6 cups hot mashed potatoes (prepared
          with milk and butter)
       2 eggs

In a saucepan, cook the beef and onion over medium heat until the meat is no longer pink; drain. Add the next nine ingredients; mix well. Bring to a boil; cook and stir for 2 minutes. Pour into an un-greased shallow 3-qt. baking dish. Combine potatoes and eggs; mix well. Drop by 1/2 cupfuls onto beef mixture.

Bake, uncovered, at 350° for 35-40 minutes or until bubbly and potatoes are lightly browned. **Yield:** 12 servings.

Hominy Beef Bake

Jean Stokes, Sacramento, California

I received this recipe from a friend more than 20 years ago and have been using it ever since. Corn chips create a tasty topping on a nicely spiced mixture of ground beef, hominy and chili. Even my meat-and-potatoes husband likes it.

       1 pound ground beef
       1 small onion, chopped
       2 garlic cloves, minced
       1 can (15-1/2 ounces) hominy, drained
       1 can (15 ounces) chili with beans
       1 can (8 ounces) tomato sauce
     1/2 cup water
       3 teaspoons chili powder
Salt and pepper to taste
       1 package (10-1/2 ounces) corn chips,
          crushed

In a large skillet, cook beef, onion and garlic over medium heat until meat is no longer pink; drain. Stir in the hominy, chili, tomato sauce, water, chili powder, salt and pepper.

Transfer to a greased 13-in. x 9-in. x 2-in. baking dish. Sprinkle with corn chips. Bake, uncovered, at 350° for 30 minutes or until heated through. **Yield:** 4-6 servings.

Crock-Pot Pizza

Julie Sterchi, Harrisburg, Illinois

Always a hit at our church dinners, this hearty casserole keeps folks coming back for more. It has all the flavor of pizza in a convenient slow cooker recipe.

       1 package (12 ounces) wide egg noodles
   1-1/2 pounds ground beef
     1/4 cup chopped onion
       1 jar (28 ounces) spaghetti sauce

    1 jar (4-1/2 ounces) sliced mushrooms,
      drained
1-1/2 teaspoons Italian seasoning
    1 package (3-1/2 ounces) sliced
      pepperoni, halved
    3 cups (12 ounces) shredded mozzarella
      cheese
    3 cups (12 ounces) shredded cheddar
      cheese

Cook noodles according to package directions. Meanwhile, in a large skillet, cook beef and onion over medium heat until meat is no longer pink; drain. Stir in spaghetti sauce, mushrooms and Italian seasoning. Drain noodles.

In a 5-qt. slow cooker coated with nonstick cooking spray, spread a third of the meat sauce. Cover with a third of the noodles and pepperoni. Sprinkle with a third of the cheeses. Repeat the layers twice.

Cover and cook on low for 3-4 hours or until heated through and the cheese is melted. **Yield:** 6-8 servings.

Meatball Sub Casserole

(Pictured above right)

Gina Harris, Seneca, South Carolina

If you like meatball subs, you'll love this tangy casserole. It's rich like the popular sandwiches but with none of the mess. Italian bread is spread with a cream cheese mixture, then topped with meatballs, spaghetti sauce and cheese.

  1/3 cup chopped green onions
  1/4 cup seasoned bread crumbs
    3 tablespoons grated Parmesan cheese
    1 pound ground beef
    1 loaf (1 pound) Italian bread, cut
      into 1-inch slices
    1 package (8 ounces) cream cheese,
      softened
  1/2 cup mayonnaise
    1 teaspoon Italian seasoning
  1/4 teaspoon pepper
    2 cups (8 ounces) shredded mozzarella
      cheese, *divided*
    1 jar (28 ounces) spaghetti sauce
    1 cup water
    2 garlic cloves, minced

In a bowl, combine onions, crumbs and Parmesan cheese. Crumble beef over mixture and mix well. Shape into 1-in. balls; place on a rack in a shallow baking pan. Bake at 400° for 15-20 minutes or until no longer pink.

Meanwhile, arrange bread slices in a single layer in an ungreased 13-in. x 9-in. x 2-in. baking dish (all of the bread might not be used). Combine cream cheese, mayonnaise, Italian seasoning and pepper; spread over the bread. Sprinkle with 1/2 cup mozzarella.

Combine sauce, water and garlic; add meatballs. Pour over cheese mixture; sprinkle with remaining mozzarella. Bake, uncovered, at 350° for 30 minutes or until heated through. **Yield:** 6-8 servings.

Editor's Note: Reduced-fat or fat-free mayonnaise is not recommended in this recipe.

Slow Cooker Suggestions

Browning and draining ground beef before adding it to the slow cooker will reduce the amount of fat in the finished dish.

It's best to follow the cooking temperature and time suggested. But generally, figure that 1 hour on high equals about 2 hours on low.

Confetti Spaghetti

(Pictured above)

Katherine Moss, Gaffney, South Carolina

Folks go back for second helpings of this hearty main dish. The combination of ground beef, noodles, cheese and a zippy tomato sauce is a crowd-pleaser.

 1 package (12 ounces) spaghetti
1-1/2 pounds ground beef
 1 medium green pepper, chopped
 1 medium onion, chopped
 1 can (14-1/2 ounces) diced tomatoes, undrained
 1 can (8 ounces) tomato sauce
 1 tablespoon brown sugar
 1 teaspoon salt
 1 teaspoon chili powder
1/2 teaspoon pepper
1/4 teaspoon garlic powder
1/8 teaspoon cayenne pepper
3/4 cup shredded cheddar cheese

Cook the spaghetti according to package directions. Meanwhile, in a large skillet, cook the beef, green pepper and onion over medium heat until the meat is no longer pink; drain. Stir in the next eight ingredients.

Drain spaghetti; add to the beef mixture. Transfer to a greased 13-in. x 9-in. x 2-in. baking dish. Cover and bake at 350° for 30 minutes. Uncover;

sprinkle with cheese. Bake 5 minutes longer or until cheese is melted. **Yield:** 12 servings.

Ground Beef Baked Beans

Louann Sherbach, Wantagh, New York

It's nice to have this casserole in the freezer for those nights when there's no time to cook.

 3 pounds ground beef
 4 cans (16 ounces *each*) pork and beans
 2 cups ketchup
 1 cup water
 2 envelopes onion soup mix
1/4 cup packed brown sugar
1/4 cup ground mustard
1/4 cup molasses
 1 tablespoon white vinegar
 1 teaspoon garlic powder
1/2 teaspoon ground cloves

In a Dutch oven, cook beef over medium heat until no longer pink; drain. Stir in the remaining ingredients; heat through. Transfer to two greased 2-qt. baking dishes. Cover and freeze one dish for up to 3 months. Cover and bake the second dish at 400° for 30 minutes. Uncover; bake 10-15 minutes longer or until bubbly. **Yield:** 2 casseroles (10-12 servings each).

To use frozen casserole: Thaw in the refrigerator. Cover and bake at 400° for 40 minutes. Uncover; bake 15-20 minutes longer or until bubbly.

Four-Cheese Lasagna

Janet Myers, Napanee, Ontario

Cheese stars in this lasagna. It can be prepared ahead of time and baked later. I sometimes double the recipe and freeze one in case of company.

 1 pound ground beef
 1 medium onion, chopped
 2 garlic cloves, minced
 1 can (28 ounces) tomatoes, undrained
 1 can (8 ounces) sliced mushrooms, drained
 1 can (6 ounces) tomato paste
 1 teaspoon salt

1 teaspoon dried oregano
1 teaspoon dried basil
1/2 teaspoon pepper
1/2 teaspoon fennel seed
1 carton (16 ounces) cottage cheese
2/3 cup grated Parmesan cheese
1/4 cup shredded mild cheddar cheese
1-1/2 cups (6 ounces) shredded mozzarella cheese, *divided*
2 eggs
1 pound lasagna noodles, cooked and drained

In a skillet, cook beef, onion and garlic over medium heat until meat is no longer pink and onion is tender; drain. In a blender, process the tomatoes until smooth. Stir into beef mixture along with mushrooms, tomato paste and seasonings; simmer 15 minutes.

In a bowl, combine cottage cheese, Parmesan, cheddar, 1/2 cup mozzarella and eggs. Spread 2 cups meat sauce in the bottom of an ungreased 13-in. x 9-in. x 2-in. baking dish. Arrange half the noodles over sauce. Spread cottage cheese mixture over noodles. Top with the remaining noodles and meat sauce.

Cover and bake at 350° for 45 minutes. Uncover; sprinkle with remaining mozzarella. Bake 15 minutes or until cheese melts. **Yield:** 12 servings.

Southwestern Casserole

(Pictured at right)

Joan Hallford, North Richland Hills, Texas

I've been making this mild family-pleasing casserole for years. It tastes wonderful, fits nicely into our budget and, best of all, makes a second one to freeze and enjoy later.

1 package (7 ounces) elbow macaroni
2 pounds ground beef
1 large onion, chopped
2 garlic cloves, minced
2 cans (14-1/2 ounces *each*) diced tomatoes, undrained
1 can (16 ounces) kidney beans, rinsed and drained
1 can (6 ounces) tomato paste
1 can (4 ounces) chopped green chilies, drained

1-1/2 teaspoons salt
1 teaspoon chili powder
1/2 teaspoon ground cumin
1/2 teaspoon pepper
2 cups (8 ounces) shredded Monterey Jack cheese
2 jalapeno peppers, seeded and chopped

Cook macaroni according to package directions. Meanwhile, in a large saucepan or Dutch oven, cook beef, onion and garlic over medium heat until meat is no longer pink; drain. Stir in the tomatoes, beans, tomato paste, chilies and seasonings. Bring to a boil. Reduce heat; simmer, uncovered, for 10 minutes. Drain macaroni; stir into beef mixture.

Transfer to two greased 2-qt. baking dishes. Top with cheese and jalapenos. Cover and bake at 375° for 30 minutes. Uncover; bake 10 minutes longer or until bubbly and heated through. Serve one casserole. Cool the second casserole; cover and freeze for up to 3 months. **Yield:** 2 casseroles (6 servings each).

To use frozen casserole: Thaw in the refrigerator for 8 hours. Cover and bake the casserole at 375° for 20-25 minutes or until heated through.

Editor's Note: When cutting or seeding hot peppers, use rubber or plastic gloves to protect your hands. Avoid touching your face.

Hearty Tortilla Casserole

(Pictured below and on page 70)

Terri Nelson, Warren, Minnesota

Being single, I often halve this recipe to yield a meal for one plus a lunch I can take to work. When co-workers remark on how good it looks, I ask them over to try it.

- 1/2 pound ground beef
- 2 tablespoons taco seasoning
- 1/3 cup water
- 1 small onion, finely chopped
- 1 to 2 Anaheim *or* Poblano chilies, roasted, peeled and finely chopped *or* 1 can (4 ounces) chopped green chilies
- 1 jalapeno pepper, seeded and finely chopped
- 1 garlic clove, minced
- 1 tablespoon vegetable oil
- 1/4 cup heavy whipping cream
- 1/8 teaspoon salt
- 4 flour tortillas (8 inches)
- 1 can (16 ounces) refried beans
- 1 cup (4 ounces) shredded Monterey Jack cheese, *divided*
- 1 cup (4 ounces) shredded cheddar cheese, *divided*

Sour cream and salsa, optional

In a skillet, cook beef over medium heat until no longer pink; drain. Add taco seasoning and water. Simmer, uncovered, for 5 minutes; remove from the heat and set aside. In a saucepan, saute onion, chilies, jalapeno and garlic in oil until tender, about 8 minutes. Stir in cream and salt. Cover and simmer for 5 minutes.

Spread 3 tablespoons sauce in an ungreased 8-in. square baking dish. Spread about 2 teaspoons sauce on each tortilla; layer with beans, beef mixture and 2 tablespoons of each kind of cheese. Roll up and place seam side down in baking dish. Top with remaining sauce. Bake, uncovered, at 350° for 25 minutes. Sprinkle with remaining cheeses; bake 5 minutes longer. Serve with sour cream and salsa if desired. **Yield:** 2-4 servings.

Editor's Note: When cutting or seeding hot peppers, use rubber or plastic gloves to protect your hands. Avoid touching your face.

Creamy Beef Lasagna

Jane Frawley, Charles Town, West Virginia

The creamy, Stroganoff-like filling in this distinctive lasagna makes it a stick-to-your-ribs entree. My family loves the delicious taste, and I appreciate that it's inexpensive to fix.

- 1-1/2 pounds ground beef
- 2 cans (15 ounces *each*) tomato sauce
- 1/4 cup chopped onion
- 2 teaspoons sugar
- 2 teaspoons salt
- 2 teaspoons Worcestershire sauce
- 1/2 teaspoon garlic salt
- 2 packages (8 ounces *each*) cream cheese, softened
- 1 cup (8 ounces) sour cream
- 1/4 cup milk
- 18 lasagna noodles, cooked and drained
- 1 cup (4 ounces) shredded cheddar cheese

Minced fresh parsley, optional

In a skillet, cook beef over medium heat until no longer pink; drain. Stir in the tomato sauce, onion, sugar, salt, Worcestershire sauce and garlic salt. In a mixing bowl, beat cream cheese, sour cream and milk until smooth.

In a greased 13-in. x 9-in. x 2-in. baking dish, layer a fourth of the meat sauce, six noodles and a third of cream cheese mixture. Repeat layers twice. Top with remaining meat sauce.

Cover and bake at 350° for 40 minutes. Uncover; sprinkle with cheddar cheese. Bake 5 minutes longer or until cheese is melted. Let stand 15 minutes before cutting. Sprinkle with parsley. **Yield:** 12 servings.

Sloppy Joe Biscuit Bake

Kelli Nothern, Colorado Springs, Colorado

This meaty mixture that's flavored with sloppy joe seasoning is covered with cheese and refrigerated biscuits for a hearty main dish.

- 1 pound ground beef
- 1 small onion, chopped
- 1 envelope sloppy joe seasoning
- 2 cups spaghetti sauce
- 1 can (8 ounces) tomato sauce
- 1 cup (4 ounces) shredded mozzarella cheese
- 1 cup (4 ounces) shredded cheddar cheese
- 1 tube (7-1/2 ounces) refrigerated buttermilk biscuits

In a large skillet, cook beef and onion over medium heat until meat is no longer pink; drain. Add sloppy joe seasoning, spaghetti sauce and tomato sauce; heat through.

Transfer to a greased 13-in. x 9-in. x 2-in. baking dish. Sprinkle with cheeses. Place biscuits randomly over the top. Bake, uncovered, at 375° for 15-20 minutes or until biscuits are golden brown. **Yield:** 4 servings.

Meaty Macaroni Bake

(Pictured above right)

Connie Helsing, Ashland, Nebraska

We go to lots of rodeos. This is an ideal casserole to make in the morning and pop into the oven when we get home.

- 1-1/2 pounds ground beef
- 1 medium onion, chopped
- 1 garlic clove, minced

- 1 jar (14 ounces) spaghetti sauce
- 1 cup water
- 1 can (8 ounces) tomato sauce
- 1 can (6 ounces) tomato paste
- 1/2 teaspoon salt
- 1/8 teaspoon pepper
- 2 eggs, beaten
- 1/4 cup vegetable oil
- 1 package (7 ounces) elbow macaroni, cooked and drained
- 2 cans (4 ounces *each*) mushroom stems and pieces, drained
- 1 cup (4 ounces) shredded mozzarella cheese
- 1/4 cup grated Parmesan cheese
- 1 cup soft bread crumbs
Additional mozzarella cheese, optional

In a large skillet, cook beef, onion and garlic over medium heat until meat is no longer pink; drain. Add spaghetti sauce, water, tomato sauce, tomato paste, salt and pepper. Bring to a boil. Reduce heat; simmer, uncovered, for 10 minutes.

In a bowl, combine the eggs, oil, macaroni, mushrooms, cheeses and bread crumbs. Spoon into a 3-qt. baking dish. Top with meat mixture. Bake, uncovered, at 350° for 30 minutes. Sprinkle with additional mozzarella cheese if desired. Let stand 10 minutes before serving. **Yield:** 6-8 servings.

a boil. Reduce heat; simmer, uncovered, for 2 minutes. Stir in the black beans and tomatoes. Simmer, uncovered, for 10 minutes.

Place two tortillas in a greased 13-in. x 9-in. x 2-in. baking dish. Spread with half of the refried beans and beef mixture; sprinkle with 1 cup cheese. Repeat layers. Top with remaining tortillas and cheese. Cover and bake at 350° for 25-30 minutes or until heated through and cheese is melted. **Yield:** 9 servings.

Slicing Lasagna

Letting lasagna stand for about 10 minutes after baking helps it "set up," making it easier to slice.

Taco Lasagna

(Pictured above)

Terri Keenan, Tuscaloosa, Alabama

If you like foods with Southwestern flair, this just might become a new favorite. Loaded with cheese, meat and beans, the layered casserole comes together in a snap. There are never any leftovers when I take this dish to potlucks.

   1 pound ground beef
1/2 cup chopped green pepper
1/2 cup chopped onion
2/3 cup water
   1 envelope taco seasoning
   1 can (15 ounces) black beans, rinsed and drained
   1 can (14-1/2 ounces) Mexican diced tomatoes, undrained
   6 flour tortillas (8 inches)
   1 can (16 ounces) refried beans
   3 cups (12 ounces) shredded Mexican cheese blend

In a large skillet, cook the beef, green pepper and onion over medium heat until meat is no longer pink; drain. Add water and taco seasoning; bring to

Kids Love It Casserole

Lou Monger, Richmond, Virginia

I haven't found any child yet who doesn't gobble this up. It combines spaghetti-like, kid-friendly ingredients plus nutritious spinach—which they never detect.

1-1/2 pounds ground beef
   1 cup chopped onion
   1 garlic clove, minced
   1 jar (14 ounces) spaghetti sauce with mushrooms
   1 can (8 ounces) tomato sauce
   1 can (6 ounces) tomato paste
3/4 cup water
   1 teaspoon Italian seasoning
1/2 teaspoon salt
Dash pepper
   1 package (7 ounces) macaroni shells, cooked and drained
   1 package (10 ounces) frozen chopped spinach, thawed and drained
   2 eggs, beaten
   1 cup (4 ounces) shredded sharp cheddar cheese
1/2 cup soft bread crumbs
1/4 cup grated Parmesan cheese

In a saucepan, cook beef, onion and garlic over medium heat until meat is no longer pink and vegetables are tender; drain. Add the next seven ingredients; bring to a boil. Reduce heat; cover and simmer for 10 minutes. Stir in macaroni, spinach, eggs, cheese and bread crumbs.

Pour into a greased 13-in. x 9-in. x 2-in. baking dish. Sprinkle with Parmesan cheese. Cover and bake at 350° for 30-35 minutes or until bubbly. Let stand for 10 minutes before serving. **Yield:** 10-12 servings.

Beefy Hash Brown Bake

Rochelle Boucher, Brooklyn, Wisconsin

A topping of french-fried onions provides a little crunch to this meaty main dish. Since this casserole is practically a meal in itself, I simply accompany it with a fruit salad and dessert.

  4 cups frozen shredded hash brown
      potatoes
  3 tablespoons vegetable oil
1/8 teaspoon pepper
  1 pound ground beef
  1 cup water
  1 envelope brown gravy mix
1/2 teaspoon garlic salt
  2 cups frozen mixed vegetables
  1 can (2.8 ounces) french-fried onions,
      divided
  1 cup (4 ounces) shredded cheddar
      cheese, *divided*

In a bowl, combine the potatoes, oil and pepper. Press into a greased 8-in. square baking dish. Bake, uncovered, at 350° for 15-20 minutes or until potatoes are thawed and set.

Meanwhile, in a saucepan, cook the beef over medium heat until no longer pink; drain. Stir in water, gravy mix and garlic salt. Bring to a boil; cook and stir for 2 minutes. Add vegetables; cook and stir for 5 minutes. Stir in half of the onions and cheese.

Pour over potatoes. Bake for 5-10 minutes. Sprinkle with remaining onions and cheese; bake 5 minutes longer or until cheese is melted. **Yield:** 4 servings.

Herbed Vegetable Medley

(Pictured at right)

Betty Blandford, Johns Island, South Carolina

If your family is resistant to eating vegetables, offer them this dish and I guarantee they'll dig right in! Eggplant, *zucchini, onion and yellow pepper are disguised in a savory, beefy tomato sauce.*

  2 pounds ground beef
  1 medium eggplant, cubed
  2 medium zucchini, cubed
  1 medium onion, chopped
  1 medium sweet yellow pepper, chopped
  3 garlic cloves, minced
  1 can (28 ounces) stewed tomatoes
  1 cup cooked rice
  1 cup (4 ounces) shredded cheddar
      cheese, *divided*
1/2 cup beef broth
1/2 teaspoon *each* dried oregano, savory
      and thyme
1/2 teaspoon salt
1/4 teaspoon pepper

In a Dutch oven, cook beef over medium heat until no longer pink; drain. Add the eggplant, zucchini, onion, yellow pepper and garlic; cook until tender. Add tomatoes, rice, 1/2 cup cheese, broth and seasonings; mix well.

Transfer to a greased 13-in. x 9-in. x 2-in. baking dish. Sprinkle with the remaining cheese. Bake, uncovered, at 350° for 30 minutes or until heated through. **Yield:** 10 servings.

Traditional Lasagna

(Pictured below)

Lorri Foockle, Granville, Illinois

My family first tasted this rich, classic lasagna at a friend's home on Christmas Eve. We were so impressed that it became our own holiday tradition as well. I also prepare it other times of the year. It's requested often by my sister's Italian in-laws—I consider that the highest compliment!

1	pound ground beef
3/4	pound bulk pork sausage
3	cans (8 ounces *each*) tomato sauce
2	cans (6 ounces *each*) tomato paste
2	garlic cloves, minced
2	teaspoons sugar
1	teaspoon Italian seasoning
1	teaspoon salt
1/2	teaspoon pepper
3	eggs
3	tablespoons minced fresh parsley
3	cups (24 ounces) small-curd cottage cheese
1	carton (8 ounces) ricotta cheese
1/2	cup grated Parmesan cheese
9	lasagna noodles, cooked and drained

6 slices provolone cheese
3 cups (12 ounces) shredded mozzarella cheese, *divided*

In a skillet, cook beef and sausage over medium heat until no longer pink; drain. Add the next seven ingredients. Simmer, uncovered, for 1 hour, stirring occasionally.

In a bowl, combine the eggs, parsley, cottage cheese, ricotta and Parmesan. Spread 1 cup of meat sauce in an ungreased 13-in. x 9-in. x 2-in. baking dish. Layer with three noodles, provolone cheese, 2 cups cottage cheese mixture, 1 cup mozzarella, three noodles, 2 cups meat sauce, remaining cottage cheese mixture and 1 cup mozzarella. Top with the remaining noodles, meat sauce and mozzarella (dish will be full).

Cover and bake at 375° for 50 minutes. Uncover; bake 20 minutes longer. Let stand 15 minutes before cutting. **Yield:** 12 servings.

Ground Beef 'n' Biscuits

Lois Hill, Trinity, North Carolina

This recipe was given to me by a good friend when I got married, and I have used it many times since. The saucy meal is family-pleasing.

1-1/2	pounds ground beef
1/2	cup chopped celery
1/2	cup chopped onion
2	tablespoons all-purpose flour
1	teaspoon salt
1/4	teaspoon dried oregano
1/8	teaspoon pepper
2	cans (8 ounces *each*) tomato sauce
1	package (10 ounces) frozen peas
1	tube (7-1/2 ounces) refrigerated buttermilk biscuits
1	cup (4 ounces) shredded cheddar cheese

In a skillet, cook beef, celery and onion over medium heat until meat is no longer pink and celery is tender; drain. Stir in the flour, salt, oregano and pepper until blended. Add tomato sauce and peas; simmer for 5 minutes. Transfer to a greased 13-in. x 9-in. x 2-in. baking dish.

Separate biscuits; arrange over beef mixture. Sprinkle with cheese. Bake, uncovered, at 350° for 20 minutes or until biscuits are golden and cheese is melted. **Yield:** 6 servings.

Zucchini Beef Lasagna

Brenda Tumasone, Newhall, California

This fresh-tasting and mildly seasoned Italian entree is a real crowd-pleaser.

- 1 pound ground beef
- 2 garlic cloves, minced
- 2 cans (8 ounces *each*) tomato sauce
- 1/2 cup water
- 1 can (6 ounces) tomato paste
- 2 bay leaves
- 1 teaspoon minced fresh parsley
- 1 teaspoon Italian seasoning
- 1 package (16 ounces) lasagna noodles, cooked, rinsed and drained
- 1 cup cottage cheese
- 1 small zucchini, sliced and cooked
- 1 cup (8 ounces) sour cream

In a skillet, cook beef and garlic over medium heat until meat is no longer pink; drain. Add tomato sauce, water, tomato paste, bay leaves, parsley and Italian seasoning; mix well. Bring to a boil; reduce heat. Simmer, uncovered, for 30-40 minutes. Discard bay leaves.

Spread 1/2 cup meat sauce in a 13-in. x 9-in. x 2-in. baking dish coated with nonstick cooking spray. Arrange five noodles over the sauce, cutting them to fit.

Spread with cottage cheese. Cover with five noodles, half the remaining meat sauce and zucchini. Cover with five noodles and sour cream. Top with remaining noodles and meat sauce.

Bake, uncovered, at 350° for 30-35 minutes or until heated through. Let stand for 15 minutes before cutting. **Yield:** 12 servings.

Cooking Ground Beef

When browning ground beef, cook over medium heat and stir often to break apart large pieces. Use a colander to drain fat and blot meat with crumpled paper towel.

Always cook ground beef until it is medium (160°) and no longer pink. The most accurate way to determine doneness in thick patties, meat loaves and meatballs is with an instant-read thermometer.

Never eat uncooked ground beef.

Mexican Manicotti

(Pictured above)

Lucy Shifton, Wichita, Kansas

I serve this hearty entree with Spanish rice, salsa and tortilla chips. I've also made it without ground beef, and our friends who are vegetarians requested the recipe.

- 1 pound ground beef
- 1 can (16 ounces) refried beans
- 2-1/2 teaspoons chili powder
- 1-1/2 teaspoons dried oregano
- 1 package (8 ounces) manicotti shells
- 2-1/2 cups water
- 1 jar (16 ounces) picante sauce
- 2 cups (16 ounces) sour cream
- 1 cup (4 ounces) shredded Mexican cheese blend
- 1/4 cup sliced green onions
- Sliced ripe olives, optional

In a bowl, combine the uncooked beef, beans, chili powder and oregano. Spoon into uncooked manicotti shells; arrange in a greased 13-in. x 9-in. x 2-in. baking dish. Combine water and picante sauce; pour over shells. Cover and refrigerate overnight.

Remove from the refrigerator 30 minutes before baking. Cover and bake at 350° for 1 hour or until meat is no longer pink. Uncover; spoon sour cream over the top. Sprinkle with cheese, onions and olives if desired. Bake 5-10 minutes longer or until the cheese is melted. **Yield:** 8 servings.

In a saucepan, melt butter. Stir in flour and salt until smooth. Gradually add milk. Bring to a boil; cook and stir for 2 minutes or until thickened. Pour over meat mixture; mix well. Sprinkle with cheese. Bake, uncovered, at 350° for 20-30 minutes or until heated through. **Yield:** 4-6 servings.

Beef Broccoli Supper

Nita Graffis, Dove Creek, Colorado

When I put together a cookbook for our family reunion, my sister submitted this recipe. My husband and our boys usually don't care for broccoli, but they enjoy it in this dish.

      3/4 cup uncooked long grain rice
        1 pound ground beef
    1-1/2 cups fresh broccoli florets
        1 can (10-3/4 ounces) condensed broccoli
           cheese soup, undiluted
      1/2 cup milk
        1 teaspoon salt-free seasoning blend
        1 teaspoon salt
      1/2 teaspoon pepper
      1/2 cup dry bread crumbs
        2 tablespoons butter, melted

Cook rice according to package directions. Meanwhile, in a large skillet, cook beef over medium heat until no longer pink; drain. Add the rice, broccoli, soup, milk, seasoning blend, salt and pepper; stir until combined. Transfer mixture to a greased 2-qt. baking dish.

Toss bread crumbs and butter; sprinkle over beef mixture. Cover and bake at 350° for 30 minutes. Uncover; bake 5-10 minutes longer or until heated through. **Yield:** 4-6 servings.

Spinach Skillet Bake

(Pictured above)

Nancy Robaidek, Krakow, Wisconsin

Over the years, I've tried to instill a love of cooking in our seven children. And we've enjoyed a variety of delicious recipes, including this one.

        1 pound ground beef
        1 medium onion, chopped
        1 package (10 ounces) frozen chopped
           spinach
        1 can (4 ounces) mushroom stems and
           pieces, drained
        1 teaspoon garlic salt
        1 teaspoon dried basil
      1/4 cup butter
      1/4 cup all-purpose flour
      1/2 teaspoon salt
        2 cups milk
        1 cup (4 ounces) shredded Monterey Jack
           or mozzarella cheese

In an ovenproof skillet, cook beef and onion over medium heat until meat is no longer pink; drain. Add the spinach, mushrooms, garlic salt and basil. Cover and cook for 5 minutes.

Choosing Bakeware

Casseroles should be made in oven-safe glass or ceramic baking dishes. Metal pans may discolor if the ingredients are acidic or may give off a metallic flavor. For best results, bake the casserole in the dish size called for in the recipe.

Cheesy Beef 'n' Rice

Gwen Bradshaw, Kennewick, Washington

This herb-seasoned casserole is one dish that all six of our kids love. Serve garlic bread and fresh spinach salad to round out the meal.

- 1 cup uncooked long grain rice
- 1 garlic clove, minced
- 2 tablespoons butter
- 3 cups water
- 2 medium carrots, shredded
- 2 teaspoons beef bouillon granules
- 1 teaspoon dried parsley flakes
- 1/2 teaspoon salt
- 1/2 teaspoon dried basil
- 1/2 teaspoon dried minced onion
- 1 pound ground beef, cooked and drained
- 1/2 cup shredded cheddar cheese

In a large saucepan, saute the rice and garlic in butter until golden brown. Stir in the water, carrots, bouillon, parsley, salt, basil and onion. Bring to a boil. Reduce heat; cover and simmer for 5 minutes. Stir in the beef.

Transfer mixture to a greased 9-in. square baking dish. Cover and bake at 325° for 45 minutes, stirring twice. Uncover; sprinkle with cheese. Bake 5 minutes longer or until the cheese is melted. **Yield:** 6 servings.

Saucy Beef Casserole

Ferne Spielvogel, Fairwater, Wisconsin

I use canned soups and crunchy chow mein noodles to flavor this hearty ground beef bake.

- 1 pound ground beef
- 1 medium onion, chopped
- 1 can (10-3/4 ounces) condensed cream of chicken soup, undiluted
- 1 can (10-3/4 ounces) condensed vegetable soup, undiluted
- 3/4 cup chow mein noodles

In a skillet, cook beef and onion over medium heat until meat is no longer pink; drain. Stir in soups. Transfer to a greased 8-in. square baking dish.

Cover and bake at 350° for 25-30 minutes or until heated through. Uncover; sprinkle with chow mein noodles. Bake 5 minutes longer or until noodles are crisp. **Yield:** 4 servings.

Tortilla Beef Bake

(Pictured below)

Kim Osburn, Ligonier, Indiana

My family loves Mexican food, so I came up with this simple, satisfying ground beef casserole that gets its spark from salsa.

- 1-1/2 pounds ground beef
- 1 can (10-3/4 ounces) condensed cream of chicken soup, undiluted
- 2-1/2 cups crushed tortilla chips, *divided*
- 1 jar (16 ounces) salsa
- 1-1/2 cups (6 ounces) shredded cheddar cheese

In a skillet, cook the beef over medium heat until no longer pink; drain. Stir in the soup. Sprinkle 1-1/2 cups tortilla chips in a greased shallow 2-1/2-qt. baking dish. Top with the beef mixture, salsa and cheese.

Bake, uncovered, at 350° for 25-30 minutes or until bubbly. Sprinkle with the remaining chips. Bake 3 minutes longer or until chips are lightly toasted. **Yield:** 6 servings.

Baked Ziti

(Pictured below)

Elaine Anderson, Aliquippa, Pennsylvania

I enjoy making this dish for family and friends. It's easy to prepare, and I like to get creative with the sauce. For example, sometimes I might add my home-canned tomatoes, mushrooms or other vegetables.

- 12 ounces uncooked ziti *or* small tube pasta
- 2 pounds ground beef
- 1 jar (28 ounces) spaghetti sauce
- 2 eggs
- 1 carton (15 ounces) ricotta cheese
- 2-1/2 cups (10 ounces) shredded mozzarella cheese, *divided*
- 1/2 cup grated Parmesan cheese

Cook pasta according to package directions. Meanwhile, in a skillet, cook beef over medium heat until no longer pink; drain. Stir in spaghetti sauce. In a bowl, combine the eggs, ricotta cheese, 1-1/2 cups mozzarella cheese and Parmesan cheese.

Drain pasta; add to cheese mixture and toss to coat. Spoon a third of the meat sauce into a greased 13-in. x 9-in. x 2-in. baking dish; top with half of the pasta mixture. Repeat layers. Top with remaining meat sauce.

Cover and bake at 350° for 40 minutes. Uncover; sprinkle with remaining mozzarella. Bake 5-10 minutes longer or until the cheese is melted. Let stand 15 minutes before serving. **Yield:** 6-8 servings.

Bacon-Colby Lasagna

Cathy McCartney, Davenport, Iowa

With both bacon and ground beef, this hearty dish is a crowd-pleaser. The recipe came from my grandmother. I've learned so much from helping her in the kitchen.

- 2 pounds ground beef
- 2 medium onions, chopped
- 2 pounds sliced bacon, cooked and crumbled
- 2 cans (15 ounces *each*) tomato sauce
- 2 cans (14-1/2 ounces *each*) diced tomatoes, undrained
- 2 tablespoons sugar
- 1 teaspoon salt
- 24 lasagna noodles, cooked and drained
- 8 cups (32 ounces) shredded Colby cheese

In a Dutch oven, cook beef and onions over medium heat until meat is no longer pink; drain. Stir in the bacon, tomato sauce, tomatoes, sugar and salt; cook until heated through.

Spread 1 cup meat sauce in each of two greased 13-in. x 9-in. x 2-in. baking dishes. Layer four noodles, 1-2/3 cups meat sauce and 1-1/3 cups cheese in each dish. Repeat layers twice.

Cover and bake at 350° for 40 minutes. Uncover; bake 5-10 minutes longer or until bubbly. Let stand for 15 minutes before cutting. **Yield:** 2 casseroles (12 servings each).

Beefy Corn Bread Casserole

Patty Boling, Seymour, Tennessee

To stretch our grocery budget, we tend to eat a lot of soups and pots o' beans. This satisfying Mexican corn bread always livens up the meal. Like many of my recipes, this one came from a church cookbook I got a number of years ago.

- 1 pound ground beef
- 1 small onion, chopped
- 2 to 3 jalapeno peppers, seeded and chopped
- 1 package (8-1/2 ounces) corn bread/muffin mix
- 3/4 teaspoon salt
- 1/2 teaspoon baking soda
- 1 can (14-3/4 ounces) cream-style corn
- 1 cup milk
- 1/2 cup vegetable oil
- 2 eggs, beaten
- 3 cups (12 ounces) shredded cheddar cheese, *divided*

In a large skillet, cook the beef, onion, and peppers over medium heat until meat is no longer pink; drain and set aside. In a small bowl, combine the corn bread mix, salt, baking soda, corn, milk, oil and eggs.

Pour half of the corn bread mixture in a greased 13-in. x 9-in. x 2-in. baking dish. Layer with half of the cheese and all of the beef mixture. Top with remaining cheese. Carefully spread remaining corn bread mixture over top.

Bake, uncovered, at 350° for 40-45 minutes or until a toothpick inserted near the center comes out clean. **Yield:** 8-12 servings.

Editor's Note: When cutting or seeding hot peppers, use rubber or plastic gloves to protect your hands. Avoid touching your face.

- 1 can (2-1/4 ounces) sliced ripe olives, drained
- 2 cups (8 ounces) shredded mozzarella cheese
- 3/4 cup biscuit/baking mix
- 2 eggs
- 3/4 cup milk

In a large skillet, cook beef and green pepper over medium heat until meat is no longer pink; drain. Stir in the pizza sauce, pepperoni and olives. Transfer to a greased 11-in. x 7-in. x 2-in. baking dish. Sprinkle with cheese.

In a small bowl, combine the biscuit mix, eggs and milk until blended. Pour evenly over cheese. Bake, uncovered, at 400° for 25-30 minutes or until golden brown. Let stand for 10 minutes before serving. **Yield:** 6 servings.

Meat Lover's Pizza Bake

(Pictured above right)

Carol Oakes, Sturgis, Michigan

This yummy pizza casserole is so hearty made with ground beef and pepperoni. Instead of a typical pizza crust, it features a crust-like topping that's a snap to make with biscuit mix.

- 1 pound ground beef
- 1/2 cup chopped green pepper
- 1 can (15 ounces) pizza sauce
- 1 package (3-1/2 ounces) sliced pepperoni, chopped

Easy Chopped Onions

To save some time in the kitchen, pick up a bag of already-chopped onions from your grocer's freezer.

One small onion equals 1/4 cup chopped. A medium onion equals 1/2 cup, and a large onion is the same as 1 cup.

Skillet Suppers

Chapter 6

Meatball Skillet Meal

(Pictured below)

Donna Smith, Victor, New York

With colorful vegetables and nicely seasoned meatballs, this tasty meal-in-one offers a lot of flavor for a little cash. Ground beef is so economical!

- 1/2 cup finely chopped fresh mushrooms
- 1/3 cup quick-cooking oats
- 2 tablespoons finely chopped green pepper
- 2 tablespoons finely chopped onion
- 2 tablespoons dried parsley flakes
- 1 teaspoon dried basil
- 1 teaspoon dried oregano
- 1/2 teaspoon dried thyme
- 1/2 teaspoon salt
- 1/4 teaspoon pepper
- 1 pound ground beef
- 4 medium carrots, sliced
- 1 small zucchini, sliced
- 1 can (14-1/2 ounces) diced tomatoes, undrained
- 4 cups hot cooked rice

In a bowl, combine the first 10 ingredients. Crumble beef over mixture and mix well. Shape into

1-1/4-in. balls.

In a skillet, cook the meatballs over medium heat until no longer pink; drain. Add the carrots and zucchini; cook for 5 minutes or until tender. Stir in the tomatoes and heat through. Serve over rice. **Yield: 6 servings.**

Ground Beef and Veggies

Pauletta Bushnell, Lebanon, Oregon

Fresh tomato and green pepper add splashes of color to this meaty main dish. It's perfect for a family dinner or as a last-minute meal for unexpected company.

- 1 pound ground beef
- 2-1/2 cups water
- 1 cup uncooked long grain rice
- 1 large onion, chopped
- 1 tablespoon beef bouillon granules
- 1/2 teaspoon ground mustard
- 8 slices cheddar *or* process American cheese, *divided*
- 1 medium green pepper, chopped
- 1 medium tomato, chopped

In a skillet, cook beef over medium heat until no longer pink; drain. Stir in water, rice, onion, bouillon and mustard. Bring to a boil; reduce heat. Cover and simmer for 20 minutes.

Cut six cheese slices into small pieces; add to rice mixture with green pepper and tomato. Cut remaining cheese slices diagonally into four triangles; arrange over top.

Cover and remove from the heat. Let stand until liquid is absorbed and cheese is melted. **Yield: 6 servings.**

Almost Stuffed Peppers

Jan Roat, Red Lodge, Montana

For a quick way to enjoy an old favorite, stir up stuffed green pepper makings in a skillet. This easy one-pan meal is requested so often I even make it when I'm not in a hurry.

- 1 pound ground beef
- 2 cups water

>   1 can (14-1/2 ounces) diced tomatoes,
>   undrained
>   1 large green pepper, cut into 1/4-inch
>   slices
>   1 medium onion, thinly sliced
> 1-1/2 teaspoons salt
>   1/2 teaspoon Italian seasoning
>   1/2 teaspoon pepper
> 1-1/2 cups uncooked instant rice

In a large skillet, cook beef over medium heat until no longer pink; drain. Set beef aside and keep warm.

In the same skillet, combine water, tomatoes, green pepper, onion and seasonings; bring to a boil. Reduce heat; simmer, uncovered, until vegetables are tender.

Stir in the rice; cover the skillet and remove from the heat. Let stand for 5 minutes. Stir in beef; return skillet to the stovetop and heat through. **Yield:** 4-6 servings.

Ground Beef Stew

Sandra Castillo, Sun Prairie, Wisconsin

I created this chunky soup when looking for something inexpensive and easy to make. The thick and hearty mixture is chock-full of ground beef, potatoes and baby carrots.

>   1 pound ground beef
>   6 medium potatoes, peeled and cubed
>   1 package (16 ounces) baby carrots
>   3 cups water
>   2 tablespoons dry onion soup mix
>   1 garlic clove, minced
>   1 teaspoon Italian seasoning
>   1 to 1-1/2 teaspoons salt
>   1/4 teaspoon garlic powder
>   1/4 teaspoon pepper
>   1 can (10-3/4 ounces) condensed tomato
>   soup, undiluted
>   1 can (6 ounces) Italian tomato paste

In a skillet, cook beef over medium heat until no longer pink; drain. In a slow cooker, combine the next nine ingredients. Stir in the beef. Cover and cook on high for 4-5 hours.

Stir in the soup and tomato paste; cover and cook for 1 hour or until heated through. **Yield:** 12 servings.

Hearty Hamburger Supper

(Pictured above)

Georgene Remm, Wausa, Nebraska

My husband and I are retired and enjoy home cooking. This hearty stovetop meal proves it need not be time-consuming. I gave this recipe to a young neighbor who tells me she uses it often since she's a nurse and is always short of time.

>   3/4 pound ground beef
>   1 small onion, chopped
>   4 cups diced cabbage
>   1/4 cup all-purpose flour
> 1-1/2 teaspoons salt
>   1/4 teaspoon paprika
>   2 cups milk
> Hot mashed potatoes
> Additional paprika

In a large saucepan, cook the beef and onion over medium heat until beef is no longer pink and onion is tender; drain. Add cabbage; cook and stir for 2 minutes. Sprinkle with flour, salt and paprika; mix well. Gradually add milk.

Bring to a boil; boil and stir for 2 minutes. Reduce heat; cover and simmer for 10-12 minutes or until the cabbage is tender. Serve over potatoes. Sprinkle with paprika if desired. **Yield:** 4 servings.

In a Dutch oven, cook cabbage in boiling water for 10 minutes or until outer leaves are tender; drain. Rinse in cold water; drain. Remove eight large outer leaves (refrigerate remaining cabbage for another use); set aside.

In a saucepan, saute 1 cup onion in butter until tender. Add the tomatoes, garlic, brown sugar and 1/2 teaspoon salt. Simmer for 15 minutes, stirring occasionally.

Meanwhile, in a bowl, combine the rice, ketchup, Worcestershire sauce, pepper and the remaining onion and salt. Add the beef and sausage and mix well.

Remove thick vein from cabbage leaves for easier rolling. Place about 1/2 cup meat mixture on each leaf; fold in sides. Starting at an unfolded edge, roll up leaf to completely enclose filling. Place seam side down in a skillet. Top with the sauce. Cover and cook over medium-low heat for 1 hour.

Add V8 juice if desired. Reduce heat to low; cook 20 minutes longer or until the cabbage rolls are heated through and the meat is no longer pink. **Yield:** 4 servings.

Classic Cabbage Rolls

(Pictured above)

Beverly Zehner, McMinnville, Oregon

I've always enjoyed cabbage rolls but didn't make them since most methods were too complicated. This recipe is fairly simple and results in the best cabbage rolls. My husband, Sid, requests them often. They're terrific to share at gatherings with our children and grandchildren.

   1 medium head cabbage, cored
1-1/2 cups chopped onion, *divided*
   1 tablespoon butter
   2 cans (14-1/2 ounces *each*) Italian stewed tomatoes
   4 garlic cloves, minced
   2 tablespoons brown sugar
1-1/2 teaspoons salt, *divided*
   1 cup cooked rice
1/4 cup ketchup
   2 tablespoons Worcestershire sauce
1/4 teaspoon pepper
   1 pound ground beef
1/4 pound bulk Italian sausage
1/2 cup V8 juice, optional

Mexican Beef and Dumplings

Sue Gronholz, Columbus, Wisconsin

My husband and I love this spicy ground beef concoction that's seasoned with chili powder. The cornmeal dumplings—which are a little "heavier" than typical dumplings—are a fun variation, and they can be stirred up in no time.

   2 pounds ground beef
   1 can (15-1/4 ounces) whole kernel corn, undrained
   1 can (14-1/2 ounces) diced tomatoes, undrained
   1 can (14-1/2 ounces) tomato sauce
   1 small onion, chopped
1/2 cup chopped celery
1/4 cup chopped green pepper
   1 tablespoon chili powder
1-1/2 teaspoons salt
DUMPLINGS:
   1 cup all-purpose flour
   1 cup cornmeal
   2 teaspoons baking powder
Pinch salt
   1 cup milk

In a Dutch oven or large kettle, cook the beef over medium heat until no longer pink; drain. Stir in the next eight ingredients. Cover and simmer for 15 minutes.

For the dumplings, combine flour, cornmeal, baking powder and salt; stir in milk. Drop eight mounds onto boiling mixture. Reduce the heat; cover and simmer for 12-15 minutes or until the dumplings test done. (Do not lift the cover while simmering.) **Yield:** 8 servings.

Cheeseburger Pancakes

Donna Wenzel, Monroe, Michigan

I combine the flavors of juicy cheeseburgers and fresh-ly baked buns in this dinner delight. Served with ketchup, a cheese sauce or cream of mushroom soup mixed with half-and-half cream, this is a hearty meal that my whole family enjoys.

  1 pound ground beef
1/2 cup chopped onion
1/2 cup chopped celery
1/4 cup chopped green pepper
  1 can (10-3/4 ounces) condensed tomato soup, undiluted
  1 teaspoon Worcestershire sauce
1/2 teaspoon celery seed
1/4 teaspoon salt
1/8 teaspoon pepper
  1 cup (4 ounces) shredded cheddar cheese
  2 cups all-purpose flour
  4 teaspoons baking powder
  1 egg
  1 cup milk

In a skillet, cook beef, onion, celery and green pepper over medium heat until meat is no longer pink and the vegetables are tender; drain. Stir in the soup, Worcestershire sauce, celery seed, salt and pepper. Remove from the heat; cool slightly. Stir in the cheese.

In a bowl, combine the flour and baking powder. Combine the egg and milk; stir into dry ingredients just until moistened. Add beef mixture and mix well.

Pour the batter by 1/4 cupfuls onto a lightly greased hot griddle. Cook for 4-6 minutes on each side or until the pancakes are golden brown. **Yield:** about 2 dozen.

Blue Plate Beef Patties

(Pictured below)

Phyllis Miller, Danville, Indiana

A friend and I discovered this recipe together and both consider it a staple menu item. I fix the moist, mild-tasting patties often for family and friends. We love them with mashed potatoes, rice or noodles and the gravy, which gets great flavor from fresh mushrooms.

    1 egg
    2 green onions with tops, sliced
 1/4 cup seasoned bread crumbs
    1 tablespoon prepared mustard
1-1/2 pounds ground beef
    1 jar (12 ounces) beef gravy
 1/2 cup water
    2 to 3 teaspoons prepared horseradish
 1/2 pound fresh mushrooms, sliced

In a bowl, beat the egg; stir in onions, bread crumbs and mustard. Crumble beef over mixture and mix well. Shape into four 1/2-in.-thick patties. In an un-greased skillet, cook patties for 4-5 minutes on each side or until meat is no longer pink; drain.

In a small bowl, combine gravy, water and horse-radish; add mushrooms. Pour over patties. Cook, uncovered, for 5 minutes or until mushrooms are tender and heated through. **Yield:** 4 servings.

Beef-Stuffed Sopaipillas

(Pictured below)

Lara Pennell, Irving, Texas

After my brothers' football games when we were kids, we would all go to a local restaurant for their wonderful Southwestern stuffed sopaipillas. This recipe takes me back to that delicious childhood memory. Even my Canadian husband raves about these!

- 2 cups all-purpose flour
- 1 teaspoon salt
- 1 teaspoon baking powder
- 1/2 cup water
- 1/4 cup evaporated milk
- 1-1/2 teaspoons vegetable oil
- Additional oil for frying
- FILLING:
- 1 pound ground beef
- 3/4 cup chopped onion
- 1/2 teaspoon salt
- 1/2 teaspoon garlic powder
- 1/4 teaspoon pepper
- SAUCE:
- 1 can (10-3/4 ounces) condensed cream of chicken soup, undiluted
- 1/2 cup chicken broth
- 1 can (4 ounces) chopped green chilies
- 1/2 teaspoon onion powder
- 2 cups (8 ounces) shredded cheddar cheese

In a bowl, combine the flour, salt and baking powder. Stir in water, milk and oil with a fork until a ball forms. On a lightly floured surface, knead dough gently for 2-3 minutes. Cover and let stand for 15 minutes. Divide into four portions; roll each into a 6-1/2-in. circle.

In an electric skillet or deep-fat fryer, heat oil to 375°. Fry circles, one at a time, for 2-3 minutes on each side or until golden brown. Drain on paper towels.

In a skillet, cook beef and onion over medium heat until meat is no longer pink; drain. Stir in the salt, garlic powder and pepper. In a saucepan, combine soup, broth, chilies and onion powder; cook for 10 minutes or until heated through.

Cut a slit on one side of each sopaipilla; fill with 1/2 cup of meat mixture. Top with cheese. Serve with sauce. **Yield:** 4 servings.

Skillet Meat Loaf

Becky Bolte, Jewell, Kansas

Meat loaf that cooks in less than half an hour? It's true! This is the best and fastest meat loaf I've ever tasted. The moist, mild slices are great served with mashed potatoes on the side.

- 2 eggs, beaten
- 1/2 cup ketchup
- 1 tablespoon Worcestershire sauce
- 1 teaspoon prepared mustard
- 1/4 teaspoon salt
- 1/4 teaspoon pepper
- 2 cups crushed saltines (about 40 crackers)
- 1 small onion, chopped
- 1/2 cup thinly sliced celery
- 1/2 cup thinly sliced carrot
- 2 pounds ground beef
- Additional ketchup and mustard, optional

In a large bowl, combine the first six ingredients. Add saltines, onion, celery and carrot. Crumble beef over mixture and mix well. Pat into a 10-in. skillet. Top with ketchup and mustard if desired.

Cover and cook over medium heat for 8 minutes.

Reduce heat to low; cover and cook 15-20 minutes longer or until meat is no longer pink and a meat thermometer reads 160°. Drain. Let stand a few minutes before serving. **Yield:** 8 servings.

Chili Nacho Supper

(Pictured at right)

Laurie Withers, Wildomar, California

The recipe for this creamy, chili-like dish was passed down through our church years ago. It's so warm and filling that we often prepare it when we take skiing trips to Colorado. It can be served over corn chips and eaten with a fork...or kept warm in a slow cooker and served as a hearty dip at parties.

2-1/2   **pounds ground beef**
  3   **cans (15 ounces *each*) tomato sauce**
  2   **cans (16 ounces *each*) pinto beans, rinsed and drained**
  1   **can (10 ounces) diced tomatoes and green chilies, undrained**
  2   **envelopes chili mix**
  2   **pounds process cheese (Velveeta), cubed**
  1   **cup heavy whipping cream**
  2   **packages (16 ounces *each*) corn chips**
Sour cream

In a Dutch oven, cook the beef over medium heat until no longer pink; drain. Add tomato sauce, beans, tomatoes and chili mix; heat through. Add cheese and cream; cook until the cheese is melted. Serve over chips. Top with sour cream. **Yield:** 14-16 servings.

Mandarin Beef Skillet

Elaine Healy, Gobles, Michigan

I've served this recipe with great success at many community gatherings. It's also a favorite of the family. Everyone likes its savory, sweet flavor.

  1   **pound ground beef**
  1   **small onion, sliced**
  1   **can (11 ounces) mandarin oranges**
1-1/2   **cups water, *divided***
  1/4   **cup soy sauce**
  3/4   **teaspoon ground ginger**
  2   **tablespoons cornstarch**
  3   **celery ribs, sliced**
  1   **small green pepper, chopped**
  1   **can (8 ounces) sliced water chestnuts, drained**
  1   **can (4 ounces) mushroom stems and pieces, drained**
Hot cooked rice

In a skillet, cook the beef and onion over medium heat until meat is no longer pink; drain. Drain the oranges, reserving syrup. Add syrup to the meat mixture and set the oranges aside. Stir in 1 cup of water, soy sauce and ginger. Cover and simmer for 5 minutes.

Combine cornstarch and remaining water until smooth; stir into meat mixture. Bring to a boil; cook and stir for 2 minutes or until thickened. Add the celery, pepper, water chestnuts and mushrooms. Cover and cook over low heat for 5-7 minutes or until heated through. Serve over rice. Garnish with the oranges. **Yield:** 4-6 servings.

Timely Tip

If you want to save time, you can make Mandarin Beef Skillet ahead and then reheat it. But don't garnish with the mandarin oranges until just before serving.

Add pepper Jack cheese and chilies to the rice. Sprinkle cheddar cheese over beef mixture; serve with rice and remaining salsa. **Yield:** 4 servings.

One-Skillet Spaghetti

Joan Shew Chuk, St. Benedict, Saskatchewan

I call this medley my "homemade Hamburger Helper." Even the pasta cooks in the same pan.

> 1 pound ground beef
> 2 medium onions, chopped
> 1 package (7 ounces) ready-cut spaghetti
> 1 can (28 ounces) diced tomatoes, undrained
> 3/4 cup chopped green pepper
> 1/2 cup water
> 1 can (8 ounces) sliced mushrooms, drained
> 1 teaspoon chili powder
> 1 teaspoon dried oregano
> 1 teaspoon sugar
> 1 teaspoon salt
> 1 cup (4 ounces) shredded cheddar cheese

In a large skillet, cook beef and onions over medium heat until meat is no longer pink; drain. Stir in uncooked spaghetti and the next eight ingredients; bring to a boil.

Reduce heat; cover and simmer for 30 minutes or until the spaghetti is tender. Sprinkle with cheese; cover and heat until melted. **Yield:** 4-6 servings.

Santa Fe Supper

(Pictured above)

Valerie Collier, Charleston, South Carolina

This zesty skillet meal is a great way to bring a little variety to your dinnertime lineup. Green chilies spice up the rice, while salsa, zucchini, onion and cheddar cheese dress up the ground beef mixture.

> 1 cup uncooked long grain rice
> 1 pound ground beef
> 2 small zucchini, cut into 1/4-inch slices
> 1 large onion, halved and sliced
> 1-1/2 cups chunky salsa, *divided*
> 1/4 teaspoon salt
> 1/4 teaspoon pepper
> 1 cup (4 ounces) shredded pepper Jack cheese
> 1 can (4 ounces) chopped green chilies, drained
> 1 cup (4 ounces) shredded cheddar cheese

Cook rice according to package directions. Meanwhile, in a large skillet, cook the beef over medium heat until no longer pink; drain. Stir in the zucchini, onion, 1 cup salsa, salt and pepper; cook until vegetables are crisp-tender.

Pantry Skillet

Susie Smith, Sauk Village, Illinois

An envelope of soup mix gives fast flavor to this beefy stovetop supper. I came up with this all-in-one dish by using whatever ingredients I had on hand.

> 1 pound ground beef
> 1 can (10-3/4 ounces) condensed tomato soup, undiluted
> 1-1/2 cups water
> 1 envelope onion mushroom soup mix
> 1/2 pound fresh mushrooms, sliced
> 1-1/2 cups frozen cut green beans
> 3 medium carrots, grated

1 cup cooked rice
2 slices process American cheese, cut into strips

In a large skillet, cook beef over medium heat until no longer pink; drain. Stir in the soup, water and soup mix; mix well. Stir in mushrooms, beans, carrots and rice. Bring to a boil. Reduce heat; cover and simmer for 5-7 minutes or until beans are tender. Top with cheese; cover and let stand until cheese is melted. **Yield:** 6 servings.

Speedy Beef Hash

Sara McCoy, Goshen, Kentucky

I rely on frozen hash browns and prepared salsa to hurry along this stovetop specialty. I'm a registered nurse who likes to spend my free time with my family, so this time-saving twist on ground beef hash is a favorite.

1 pound ground beef
1 medium onion, chopped
3 cups frozen O'Brien hash brown potatoes, thawed
1/2 teaspoon salt
1/4 teaspoon pepper
1 cup salsa
1/2 cup shredded Colby-Monterey Jack cheese
Sliced green onions and ripe olives, optional

In a skillet, cook beef and onion over medium heat until the meat is no longer pink; drain. Stir in the potatoes, salt and pepper.

Cook and stir over medium-high heat for 7-9 minutes or until potatoes are lightly browned. Stir in salsa. Sprinkle with cheese; cook until melted. Sprinkle with onions and olives if desired. **Yield:** 4 servings.

Meaty Mac 'n' Cheese

(Pictured at right)

Charlotte Kremer, Pahrump, Nevada

My husband is disabled and requires constant care. This doesn't leave me a lot of time to cook, so I came up with this tasty way to beef up a box of macaroni and cheese. The hearty mixture gets extra flavor from corn, ripe olives and zippy salsa.

1 package (7-1/4 ounces) macaroni and cheese
1 pound ground beef
1/4 cup chopped onion
1-1/2 cups salsa
1/2 cup fresh *or* frozen corn
1 can (2-1/4 ounces) sliced ripe olives, drained
3 tablespoons diced pimientos
Shredded cheddar cheese
Chopped tomato

Set aside cheese sauce mix from macaroni and cheese; cook macaroni according to package directions. Meanwhile, in a large saucepan, cook beef and onion over medium heat until meat is no longer pink; drain.

Add the salsa, corn, olives and pimientos; heat through. Drain macaroni; add to beef mixture with contents of cheese sauce mix. Mix well; heat through. Garnish with cheese and tomato. **Yield:** 4-6 servings.

Editor's Note: The milk and butter listed on the macaroni and cheese package are not used in this recipe.

South Seas Skillet

(Pictured below)

Bernice Muilenburg, Molalla, Oregon

Soy sauce, raisins, water chestnuts and toasted almonds lend to this dish's tropical flavor. Served over rice, it's a filling entree that satisfies my family.

  1 **pound ground beef**
  1 **package (10 ounces) frozen peas**
  1 **can (8 ounces) sliced water chestnuts, drained**
  2 **jars (4-1/2 ounces** *each***) sliced mushrooms, drained**
1/2 **cup beef broth**
1/2 **cup golden raisins**
1/2 **cup soy sauce**
  2 **teaspoons ground ginger**
1/2 **cup slivered almonds, toasted**
Fresh orange slices
Hot cooked rice

In a skillet, cook beef over medium heat until no longer pink; drain. Add peas, water chestnuts, mushrooms, broth, raisins, soy sauce and ginger; mix well. Bring to a boil. Reduce heat; cover and simmer for 15 minutes or until vegetables are tender. Garnish with almonds and orange slices. Serve over rice. **Yield:** 6-8 servings.

Colorful Hamburger Rice

Drusila Luckey, Marathon, New York

With a pretty blend of vegetables, this skillet dish is an eye-catching addition to a potluck buffet. You can use garden-fresh vegetables instead of frozen.

  3 **cups water**
  1 **pound ground beef, cooked and drained**
  1 **medium onion, chopped**
  2 **celery ribs, thinly sliced**
  2 **medium carrots, sliced**
  1 **cup** *each* **frozen corn, peas and cut green beans**
  1 **tablespoon butter**
  1 **teaspoon salt**
1/2 **teaspoon celery salt**
1/2 **teaspoon garlic powder**
1/4 **teaspoon pepper**
1-1/2 **cups uncooked long grain rice**
Shredded Parmesan cheese

In a large saucepan, combine the water, beef, vegetables, butter and seasonings. Bring to a boil. Add the rice. Reduce heat; cover and simmer for 20 minutes or until rice is tender. Fluff with a fork. Sprinkle with Parmesan cheese. **Yield:** 8-10 servings.

Barley Burger Stew

Judy McCarthy, Derby, Kansas

I found this hearty stew recipe in an old cookbook purchased at a flea market. The blend of beef and barley really hits the spot on cool days.

1/2 **pound ground beef**
  1 **small onion, chopped**
1/4 **cup chopped celery**
2-1/4 **cups tomato juice**
1/2 **cup water**
1/4 **cup medium pearl barley**
  1 **to 1-1/2 teaspoons chili powder**

1/2 teaspoon salt
1/4 teaspoon pepper

In a saucepan, cook beef, onion and celery over medium heat until meat is no longer pink; drain. Stir in tomato juice, water, barley, chili powder, salt and pepper. Bring to a boil. Reduce heat; cover and simmer for 50-60 minutes or until barley is tender. **Yield:** 2 servings.

Pepper Beef with Cashews

Sharon Wolf, Camrose, Alberta

I created this recipe after seeing an Oriental version of pepper steak. The pretty peppers make this dish look so attractive and create a sweet contrast to the peppery ground beef.

1-1/2 pounds ground beef
   2 teaspoons coarsely ground pepper
   1 small onion, chopped
   2 garlic cloves, minced
   4 tablespoons beef broth, *divided*
   1 *each* large sweet red, yellow and green pepper, chopped
   2 tablespoons oyster sauce, optional
   1 tablespoon soy sauce
   2 teaspoons cornstarch
 3/4 cup cashew halves

In a skillet, cook beef and pepper over medium heat until no longer pink. Remove with a slotted spoon and keep warm. Add onion and garlic to skillet; saute for 2 minutes. Add 2 tablespoons broth; mix well. Stir in the peppers. Cover and steam for 1 minute.

Return beef to pan. Stir in oyster sauce if desired and soy sauce. Combine cornstarch with remaining broth until smooth; gradually add to skillet. Bring to a boil. Cook and stir for 2 minutes or until thickened. Stir in cashews. **Yield:** 6 servings.

Baltimore Hash

(Pictured above right)

Betty Cannell, Reading, Pennsylvania

My mother-in-law created this recipe while living in Baltimore. I make many batches of it with our garden

vegetables and freeze it in serving-size portions for later. It's handy to just pull it out and heat up on a hectic weeknight.

 1 pound ground beef
 1 small onion, diced
 1 can (28 ounces) diced tomatoes, undrained
 1 cup diced carrots
 1 cup diced celery
 1 cup cubed peeled potatoes
Salt and pepper to taste

In a skillet, cook beef and onion over medium heat until meat is no longer pink; drain. Add tomatoes, carrots, celery and potatoes. Bring to a boil. Reduce heat; cover and simmer for 30 minutes or until vegetables are tender. Sprinkle with salt and pepper. **Yield:** 4-6 servings.

Simple Solution

The canned diced tomatoes in Baltimore Hash can be replaced with a quart of fresh tomatoes that have been peeled and diced. A tomato peel can be loosened in the microwave by heating the tomato on high for 15 seconds; let stand 1 minute before peeling.

In a bowl, combine egg, bread crumbs, chopped onion, salt, marjoram and thyme. Crumble beef over mixtue and mix well. Shape into 48 meatballs.

In a Dutch oven, brown meatballs in oil; drain. Add broth, soup, potatoes, carrots and pearl onions; bring to a boil. Reduce heat; simmer for 30 minutes or until the vegetables are tender and meat is no longer pink. Sprinkle with parsley. **Yield:** 8 servings.

Meatball Stew

(Pictured above)

Teresa Ingebrand, Perham, Minnesota

The combination of tender meatballs plus potatoes, carrots and pearl onions in a golden gravy really hit the spot on chilly days after we'd worked up an appetite doing our morning chores. Mom served it with pride for many wonderful Saturday dinners when I was growing up on the farm.

      1 egg, beaten
      1 cup soft bread crumbs
   1/4 cup finely chopped onion
      1 teaspoon salt
      1 teaspoon dried marjoram
   1/2 teaspoon dried thyme
1-1/2 pounds ground beef
      2 tablespoons vegetable oil
      2 cans (14-1/2 ounces *each*) beef broth
      2 cans (10-3/4 ounces *each*) condensed
          golden mushroom soup, undiluted
      4 medium potatoes, peeled and quartered
      4 medium carrots, cut into chunks
      1 jar (16 ounces) whole pearl onions,
          drained
   1/4 cup minced fresh parsley

German Skillet

Peggy Heitzman, Geneseo, Illinois

Sauerkraut lovers enjoy hearty helpings of this dish. I've been preparing this recipe for more than 20 years...we have yet to tire of it!

      3 tablespoons butter
      1 can (27 ounces) sauerkraut, rinsed and
          drained
   2/3 cup uncooked long grain rice
      1 large onion, diced
      2 pounds ground beef
1-1/2 teaspoons salt
Pepper to taste
      2 cups water
      1 can (8 ounces) tomato sauce

In a skillet, melt butter. Layer with sauerkraut, rice, onion and beef. Sprinkle with salt and pepper. In a bowl, combine water and tomato sauce; mix well. Pour over beef mixture.

Bring to a boil. Reduce heat; cover and simmer for 50 minutes or until meat is no longer pink and rice is tender (do not stir). **Yield:** 8 servings.

Spanish Noodles 'n' Ground Beef

Kelli Jones, Perris, California

Bacon adds flavor to this comforting stovetop supper my mom frequently made when we were growing up. Now I prepare it for my family. It disappears quickly and is budget-pleasing, too.

      1 pound ground beef
      1 small green pepper, chopped
      1 small onion, chopped

3-1/4 cups uncooked medium egg noodles
1 can (14-1/2 ounces) diced tomatoes, undrained
1 cup water
1/4 cup chili sauce
1 teaspoon salt
1/8 teaspoon pepper
4 bacon strips, cooked and crumbled

In a large skillet, cook the beef, green pepper and onion over medium heat until meat is no longer pink; drain. Stir in noodles, tomatoes, water, chili sauce, salt and pepper; mix well.

Cover and cook over low heat for 15-20 minutes or until the noodles are tender, stirring frequently. Add bacon. **Yield:** 5 servings.

Hamburger Stroganoff

Aline Christenot, Chester, Montana

I've been making this simple yet satisfying dish for more than 25 years. I once tried freezing the ground beef mixture so I'd have a head start on a future dinner. It works great!

1 pound ground beef
1/4 cup chopped onion
1 garlic clove, minced
1 can (10-1/2 ounces) condensed beef consomme, undiluted
1 can (4 ounces) mushroom stems and pieces, undrained
3 tablespoons lemon juice
1/4 teaspoon pepper
ADDITIONAL INGREDIENTS (for each dish):
2 cups cooked spiral pasta
1/2 cup sour cream
2 tablespoons water

In a skillet, cook beef, onion and garlic over medium heat until meat is no longer pink; drain. Stir in consomme, mushrooms, lemon juice and pepper. Place half of the mixture in a freezer container; cover and freeze for up to 3 months.

To the remaining meat mixture, add the cooked pasta, sour cream and water. Heat through but do not boil. **Yield:** 2 main dishes (2 servings each).

To use frozen meat mixture: Thaw in the refrigerator overnight. Place in a saucepan or skillet and prepare as directed.

Onion Salisbury Steak

(Pictured below and on page 88)

Claudine Moffatt, Manchester, Missouri

I've relied on this recipe for as long as I can remember. Ground beef patties, tender onion slices and a rich gravy top toasted bread to make this Depression-era favorite.

1 pound ground beef
1/2 teaspoon salt
1/8 to 1/4 teaspoon pepper
2 medium onions, thinly sliced
4 slices bread, toasted
1/4 cup all-purpose flour
1-1/2 cups water
1 tablespoon beef bouillon granules

In a bowl, combine beef, salt and pepper; shape into four oval patties. In a skillet, brown patties on one side. Turn and add onions. Cook until meat is no longer pink. Place toast on serving plates. Top each with onions and a beef patty; keep warm.

Stir flour into skillet until blended. Gradually add water; stir in bouillon. Bring to a boil; cook and stir for 2 minutes or until thickened and bubbly. Serve over meat and onions. **Yield:** 4 servings.

Garden Skillet

(Pictured below)

GaleLynn Peterson, Long Beach, California

As part of our final exam in a gourmet cooking class I took a number of years ago, we had to improve upon an existing recipe and serve it to the other students. This was my class-approved creation.

  2 **pounds ground beef**
  3 **medium zucchini, julienned**
  4 **medium carrots, julienned**
  1 **can (16 ounces) bean sprouts, drained**
  1 **medium onion, cut into thin wedges**
3/4 **cup julienned green pepper**
  1 **garlic clove, minced**
  1 **medium tomato, cut into wedges**
  1 **teaspoon salt**
  1 **teaspoon ground cumin**

In a skillet, cook beef over medium heat until no longer pink; drain. Add the zucchini, carrots, bean sprouts, onion, green pepper and garlic. Cook

and stir for 3-4 minutes or until crisp-tender. Add the tomato, salt and cumin. Cook 2 minutes longer or until heated through. **Yield:** 6-8 servings.

Bacon Cheeseburger Pasta

Melissa Stevens, Elk River, Minnesota

I start the pasta boiling first. While the noodles cook, I cook the ground beef and crisp the bacon. Then I combine the meat, tomato soup and pasta, heat through and sprinkle with cheese for a dish that's a snap to make yet is very filling.

  8 **ounces uncooked tube *or* spiral pasta**
  1 **pound ground beef**
  6 **bacon strips, diced**
  1 **can (10-3/4 ounces) condensed tomato soup, undiluted**
  1 **cup (4 ounces) shredded cheddar cheese**
Barbecue sauce and prepared mustard, optional

Cook the pasta according to the package directions. Meanwhile, in a skillet, cook the beef over medium heat until no longer pink; drain and set aside. In the same skillet, cook bacon until crisp; remove with a slotted spoon to paper towels. Discard drippings.

Drain pasta; add to the skillet. Add soup, beef and bacon; heat through. Sprinkle with cheese; cover and cook until the cheese is melted. Serve with barbecue sauce and mustard if desired. **Yield:** 4-6 servings.

Ranchero Supper

Karen Roberts, Lawrence, Kansas

This hearty dish is quick and easy to fix after a busy workday. We like to use hickory and bacon baked beans and serve it with fresh fruit or a green salad for a complete meal.

1-1/2 **pounds ground beef**
    1 **can (28 ounces) baked beans**
    1 **can (11 ounces) whole kernel corn, drained**
  1/4 **cup barbecue sauce**

2 tablespoons ketchup
1 tablespoon prepared mustard
3/4 cup shredded cheddar cheese
Sliced green onions and sour cream, optional
7 cups tortilla chips

In a large skillet, cook beef over medium heat until no longer pink; drain. Stir in the baked beans, corn, barbecue sauce, ketchup and mustard; heat through.

Sprinkle with cheese; cook until melted. Top with onions and sour cream if desired. Serve with tortilla chips. **Yield:** 7 servings.

Skillet Beef 'n' Rice

Lori Thompson, New London, Texas

Even picky children enjoy this inexpensive dish. Our kids agree it's one of their favorites and with six ingredients, it'll be ready in a snap!

1 package (6.8 ounces) beef-flavored rice mix
1 pound ground beef
1 small onion, chopped
1 small green pepper, chopped
2 tablespoons plus 1-1/2 teaspoons Worcestershire sauce
1 teaspoon garlic powder

Cook rice mix according to package directions. Meanwhile, in a large skillet, cook the beef, onion and green pepper over medium heat until the meat is no longer pink; drain. Stir in the rice mixture, Worcestershire sauce and garlic powder; mix well. **Yield:** 4 servings.

Minestrone Macaroni

(Pictured above right)

Diane Varner, Elizabeth, Colorado

This is by far the easiest, tastiest and most economical recipe I've found. It seems even better as a leftover.

1 pound ground beef
2 cans (14-1/2 ounces *each*) Italian diced tomatoes, undrained

2-1/4 cups water
1-1/2 cups uncooked elbow macaroni
2 beef bouillon cubes
1 can (16 ounces) kidney beans, rinsed and drained
1 can (15 ounces) garbanzo beans, rinsed and drained
1 can (14-1/2 ounces) cut green beans, rinsed and drained

In a large skillet, cook beef over medium heat until no longer pink; drain. Add tomatoes, water, macaroni and bouillon; bring to a boil. Reduce heat; cover and simmer for 12-15 minutes or until macaroni is tender. Stir in beans and heat through. **Yield:** 6 servings.

Storing Pasta

Dried pasta can be stored indefinitely in an airtight container in a cool dry place. Fresh or refrigerated pasta should be put in an airtight container in the refrigerator for up to 5 days.

cheese. Cover and cook 3-5 minutes longer or until cheese is melted. **Yield:** 4 servings.

Hamburger Supper

(Pictured above)

Andrea Brandt, Newton, Kansas

I have good memories of eating this meal-in-one while growing up. Instead of sprinkling it with cheddar, I sometimes create a cheese sauce using American cheese and milk. It makes it so cheesy!

> 1 pound ground beef
> 1-1/2 cups water
> 1/2 teaspoon poultry seasoning
> 1/4 teaspoon pepper
> 1 envelope brown gravy mix
> 1 medium onion, sliced and separated into rings
> 1 medium carrot, sliced
> 2 medium potatoes, sliced
> 1 cup (4 ounces) shredded cheddar cheese

In a large skillet, cook the beef over medium heat until no longer pink; drain. Stir in the water, poultry seasoning and pepper. Bring to a boil. Stir in the gravy mix. Cook and stir for 2 minutes or until slightly thickened.

Arrange the onion, carrot and potatoes over beef. Reduce heat; cover and simmer for 10-15 minutes or until vegetables are tender. Sprinkle with

Ground Beef Gravy

Sandy McKenzie, Braham, Minnesota

For an old-fashioned stick-to-your-ribs meal, try this economical entree. As a newlywed, I was so grateful to my mom for sharing this speedy recipe. My husband enjoys this no matter how often I serve it.

> 1 pound ground beef
> 1 can (10-3/4 ounces) condensed cream of mushroom soup, undiluted
> 1/2 cup milk
> 1 can (4 ounces) mushroom stems and pieces, drained
> 1-1/2 teaspoons beef bouillon granules
> 3 cups hot cooked mashed potatoes

In a large skillet, cook beef over medium heat until no longer pink; drain. Stir in the soup, milk, mushrooms and bouillon. Reduce heat. Simmer, uncovered, for 10-15 minutes or until heated through, stirring occasionally. Serve over mashed potatoes. **Yield:** 4 servings.

Western Skillet

Carol Trussler, Petersburg, Ontario

Onion soup mix accents the flavor of this easy beef-and-rice combo. Feel free to replace the frozen peas with corn or green beans, or use Swiss cheese instead of shredded cheddar cheese.

> 1 pound ground beef
> 3 cups water
> 1 can (14-1/2 ounces) stewed tomatoes
> 1-1/2 cups uncooked long grain rice
> 1 cup frozen peas, thawed
> 1 envelope onion soup mix
> 1 cup (4 ounces) shredded cheddar cheese

In a large skillet, cook beef over medium heat until no longer pink; drain. Stir in the water, tomatoes, rice, peas and soup mix. Bring to a boil. Reduce heat; cover and simmer for 25 minutes or until rice is tender. Sprinkle with cheese. **Yield:** 4-6 servings.

Skillet Enchiladas

Regina Stock, Topeka, Kansas

My family loves anything in a flour tortilla, and this is no exception. These meaty enchiladas are a snap to fix.

    2 pounds ground beef, *divided*
    1 small onion, chopped
    1 can (10-3/4 ounces) condensed cream
       of mushroom soup, undiluted
    1 can (10 ounces) enchilada sauce
  1/2 cup milk
    1 can (4 ounces) chopped green chilies
  3/4 cup water
    1 envelope taco seasoning
    8 flour tortillas (7 inches), warmed
2-1/2 cups (10 ounces) shredded cheddar
       cheese, *divided*

In a large skillet, cook 1 pound of beef and onion over medium heat until no longer pink; drain. Stir in the soup, enchilada sauce, milk and chilies. Bring to a boil. Reduce heat; simmer, uncovered, for 20 minutes, stirring occasionally.

Meanwhile, in another skillet, cook remaining beef over medium heat until no longer pink; drain. Stir in the water and taco seasoning. Bring to a boil. Reduce heat; simmer for 5 minutes, stirring occasionally.

Place about 1/4 cup taco-seasoned beef down the center of each tortilla; top with 1/4 cup cheese. Roll up and place seam side down over meat sauce in skillet. Sprinkle with remaining cheese. Cover and cook for 1-2 minutes or until cheese is melted. **Yield:** 8 servings.

Spaghetti Squash With Meat Sauce

(Pictured at right)

Lina Vainauskas, Shaw Air Force Base, South Carolina

Neither my mother nor I had tried spaghetti squash before, so when we cooked this recipe together, all we could do was grin and say, "Wow!" It's fun to separate the noodle-like strands from the squash shell, but the eating is the best part!

    1 medium spaghetti squash (about 8 inches)
    1 cup water
    1 pound ground beef

    1 large onion, chopped
    1 medium green pepper, chopped
    1 teaspoon garlic powder
    2 teaspoons dried basil
1-1/2 teaspoons dried oregano
    1 teaspoon salt
  1/2 teaspoon pepper
  1/4 to 1/2 teaspoon chili powder
    1 can (28 ounces) tomato puree
    1 cup grated Parmesan cheese, *divided*

Slice the squash lengthwise and scoop out seeds. Place squash, cut side down, in a baking dish. Add water and cover tightly with foil. Bake at 375° for 20-30 minutes or until easily pierced with a fork.

Meanwhile, cook beef in a large skillet until no longer pink; drain. Add onion, green pepper and seasonings; saute until onion is transparent. Stir in tomato puree. Cover and cook over low heat, stirring occasionally.

Scoop out the squash, separating the strands with a fork. Just before serving; stir 1/2 cup Parmesan cheese into the meat sauce. Serve sauce over spaghetti squash and serve with remaining Parmesan. **Yield:** 6 servings.

General Recipe Index

Alphabetical Index